Table of Contents Grade 1

Table of Contents, continued

Chapter 6   Geometry

Chapters 1–6 Final Test

SPECTRUM®

Math

Grade 1

Published by Spectrum®
an imprint of Carson-Dellosa Publishing
Greensboro, NC

Spectrum®
An imprint of Carson-Dellosa Publishing LLC
PO Box 35665
Greensboro, NC 27425 USA

ISBN 978-1-4838-0869-7

04-168197784

Check What You Know

Addition and Subtraction Facts through 10

Add.

$$\begin{array}{cc} 5 \\ +1 \\ \hline \end{array} \qquad \begin{array}{cc} 3 \\ +2 \\ \hline \end{array} \qquad \begin{array}{cc} 1 \\ +1 \\ \hline \end{array} \qquad \begin{array}{cc} 2 \\ +4 \\ \hline \end{array} \qquad \begin{array}{cc} 6 \\ +0 \\ \hline \end{array} \qquad \begin{array}{cc} 4 \\ +1 \\ \hline \end{array}$$

$$\begin{array}{cc} 4 \\ +0 \\ \hline \end{array} \qquad \begin{array}{cc} 2 \\ +1 \\ \hline \end{array} \qquad \begin{array}{cc} 3 \\ +0 \\ \hline \end{array} \qquad \begin{array}{cc} 1 \\ +3 \\ \hline \end{array} \qquad \begin{array}{cc} 4 \\ +2 \\ \hline \end{array} \qquad \begin{array}{cc} 1 \\ +2 \\ \hline \end{array}$$

$0 + 6 =$ _____ $3 + 3 =$ _____ $0 + 4 =$ _____

$3 + 1 =$ _____ $2 + 4 =$ _____ $1 + 5 =$ _____

Subtract.

$$\begin{array}{cc} 6 \\ -1 \\ \hline \end{array} \qquad \begin{array}{cc} 4 \\ -2 \\ \hline \end{array} \qquad \begin{array}{cc} 3 \\ -1 \\ \hline \end{array} \qquad \begin{array}{cc} 5 \\ -3 \\ \hline \end{array} \qquad \begin{array}{cc} 2 \\ -0 \\ \hline \end{array} \qquad \begin{array}{cc} 4 \\ -1 \\ \hline \end{array}$$

$$\begin{array}{cc} 5 \\ -2 \\ \hline \end{array} \qquad \begin{array}{cc} 6 \\ -4 \\ \hline \end{array} \qquad \begin{array}{cc} 2 \\ -1 \\ \hline \end{array} \qquad \begin{array}{cc} 3 \\ -2 \\ \hline \end{array} \qquad \begin{array}{cc} 6 \\ -5 \\ \hline \end{array} \qquad \begin{array}{cc} 5 \\ -0 \\ \hline \end{array}$$

$4 - 3 =$ _____ $6 - 2 =$ _____ $5 - 4 =$ _____

$6 - 3 =$ _____ $1 - 0 =$ _____ $2 - 2 =$ _____

NAME _____

Check What You Know

Addition and Subtraction Facts through 10

Solve each problem.

There are 2 [house].

There are 4 [doghouse].

How many in all? _____

Jeff has 4 [football].

Karen has 1 [football].

What is the difference? _____

There are 5 [butterfly].

3 [butterfly] fly away.

Subtract 5 minus 3. _____

There is 1 [pencil].

There are 2 [pen].

Add 1 plus 2. _____

Check What You Know

Addition and Subtraction Facts through 10

Add.

9 +1	2 +7	6 +4	0 +8	5 +3	1 +6
4 +4	0 +9	3 +6	2 +8	7 +3	3 +4
10 +0	1 +4	2 +5	8 +1	5 +5	6 +2

Subtract.

10 −5	10 −8	9 −3	8 −6	7 −1	9 −0
8 −7	10 −3	7 −7	9 −5	8 −1	7 −4
10 −1	9 −8	8 −4	10 −2	7 −0	10 −9

NAME _____

Check What You Know

SHOW YOUR WORK

Addition and Subtraction Facts through 10

Solve each problem.

There are 4 🐰.

5 more 🐰 come.

Now how many are here? _____

There are 9 🍃.

There are 6 🍁.

How many more 🍃 than 🍁 are there? _____

Miguel has 10¢.

He buys 🐛 for 7¢.

How much money does he have left? _____ ¢

Jenny has 5 🌼.

She finds 2 more 🌸.

What is the sum of 5 plus 2? _____

There are 8 🐿.

3 🐿 ran away.

What is 8 minus 3? _____

I buy ✏ for 4¢.

I buy 🖊 for 6¢.

How much money did I spend? _____ ¢

Lesson 1.1 Adding through 3

Add.

$1 + 1 = \underline{2}$ $\begin{array}{r} 1 \\ +1 \\ \hline 2 \end{array}$

one plus one equals two

$2 + 1 = \underline{}$ $\begin{array}{r} 2 \\ +1 \\ \hline \end{array}$

$1 + 2 = \underline{}$ $\begin{array}{r} 1 \\ +2 \\ \hline \end{array}$

$1 + 0 = \underline{}$ $\begin{array}{r} 1 \\ +0 \\ \hline \end{array}$

$2 + 0 = \underline{}$ $\begin{array}{r} 2 \\ +0 \\ \hline \end{array}$

$0 + 1 = \underline{}$ $\begin{array}{r} 0 \\ +1 \\ \hline \end{array}$

$0 + 2 = \underline{}$ $\begin{array}{r} 0 \\ +2 \\ \hline \end{array}$

$3 + 0 = \underline{}$ $\begin{array}{r} 3 \\ +0 \\ \hline \end{array}$

$0 + 0 = \underline{}$ $\begin{array}{r} 0 \\ +0 \\ \hline \end{array}$

$0 + 3 = \underline{}$ $\begin{array}{r} 0 \\ +3 \\ \hline \end{array}$

Lesson 1.2 Subtracting from 1, 2, and 3

Subtract.

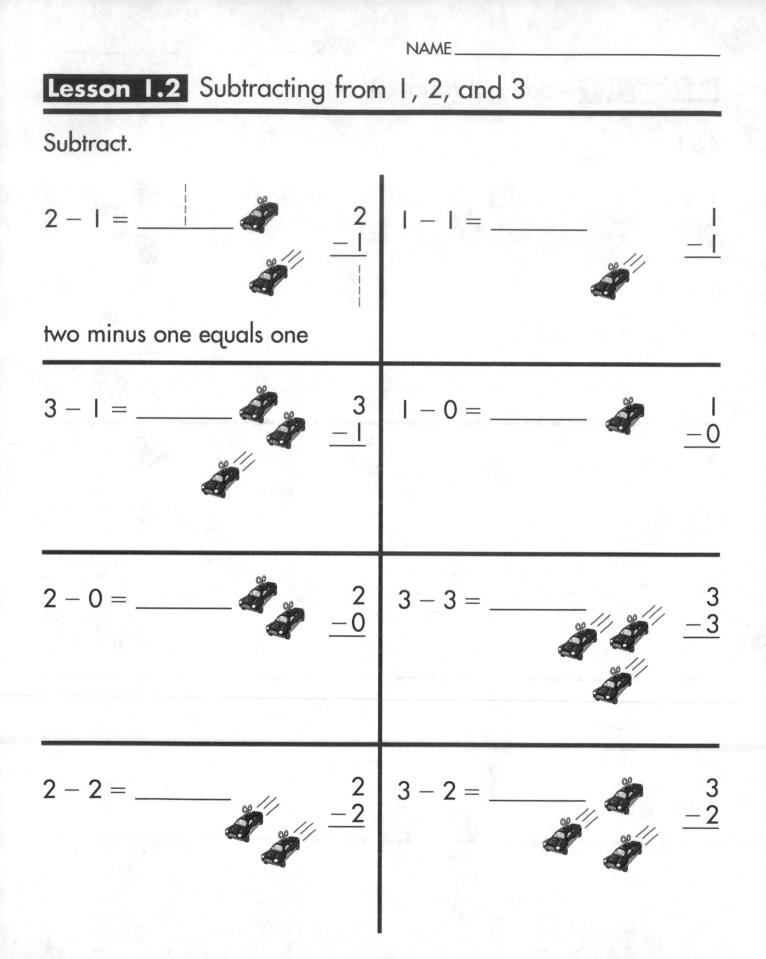

$2 - 1 =$ _____

$\begin{array}{r} 2 \\ -1 \\ \hline \end{array}$

two minus one equals one

$1 - 1 =$ _____

$\begin{array}{r} 1 \\ -1 \\ \hline \end{array}$

$3 - 1 =$ _____

$\begin{array}{r} 3 \\ -1 \\ \hline \end{array}$

$1 - 0 =$ _____

$\begin{array}{r} 1 \\ -0 \\ \hline \end{array}$

$2 - 0 =$ _____

$\begin{array}{r} 2 \\ -0 \\ \hline \end{array}$

$3 - 3 =$ _____

$\begin{array}{r} 3 \\ -3 \\ \hline \end{array}$

$2 - 2 =$ _____

$\begin{array}{r} 2 \\ -2 \\ \hline \end{array}$

$3 - 2 =$ _____

$\begin{array}{r} 3 \\ -2 \\ \hline \end{array}$

Lesson 1.3 Adding to 4 and 5

Add.

$2 + 3 =$ _____ $\begin{array}{r} 2 \\ +3 \\ \hline \end{array}$

$3 + 2 =$ _____ $\begin{array}{r} 3 \\ +2 \\ \hline \end{array}$

$2 + 2 =$ _____ $\begin{array}{r} 2 \\ +2 \\ \hline \end{array}$

$1 + 3 =$ _____ $\begin{array}{r} 1 \\ +3 \\ \hline \end{array}$

$3 + 1 =$ _____ $\begin{array}{r} 3 \\ +1 \\ \hline \end{array}$

$5 + 0 =$ _____ $\begin{array}{r} 5 \\ +0 \\ \hline \end{array}$

$0 + 5 =$ _____ $\begin{array}{r} 0 \\ +5 \\ \hline \end{array}$

$0 + 4 =$ _____ $\begin{array}{r} 0 \\ +4 \\ \hline \end{array}$

$4 + 0 =$ _____ $\begin{array}{r} 4 \\ +0 \\ \hline \end{array}$

$4 + 1 =$ _____ $\begin{array}{r} 4 \\ +1 \\ \hline \end{array}$

$1 + 4 =$ _____ $\begin{array}{r} 1 \\ +4 \\ \hline \end{array}$

Lesson 1.4 Adding to 6

Add.

$4 + 2 = \underline{}$

$\begin{array}{r} 4 \\ +2 \\ \hline \end{array}$

$5 + 1 = \underline{}$

$\begin{array}{r} 5 \\ +1 \\ \hline \end{array}$

$2 + 4 = \underline{}$

$\begin{array}{r} 2 \\ +4 \\ \hline \end{array}$

$1 + 5 = \underline{}$

$\begin{array}{r} 1 \\ +5 \\ \hline \end{array}$

$6 + 0 = \underline{}$

$\begin{array}{r} 6 \\ +0 \\ \hline \end{array}$

$3 + 3 = \underline{}$

$\begin{array}{r} 3 \\ +3 \\ \hline \end{array}$

$0 + 6 = \underline{}$

$\begin{array}{r} 0 \\ +6 \\ \hline \end{array}$

$\begin{array}{r} 3 \\ +3 \\ \hline \end{array}$
$\begin{array}{r} 4 \\ +2 \\ \hline \end{array}$
$\begin{array}{r} 3 \\ +2 \\ \hline \end{array}$
$\begin{array}{r} 5 \\ +1 \\ \hline \end{array}$
$\begin{array}{r} 0 \\ +6 \\ \hline \end{array}$
$\begin{array}{r} 1 \\ +4 \\ \hline \end{array}$

$2 + 3 = \underline{}$ $1 + 5 = \underline{}$ $3 + 3 = \underline{}$

$6 + 0 = \underline{}$ $2 + 4 = \underline{}$ $1 + 3 = \underline{}$

Lesson 1.5 Subtracting from 4 and 5

Subtract.

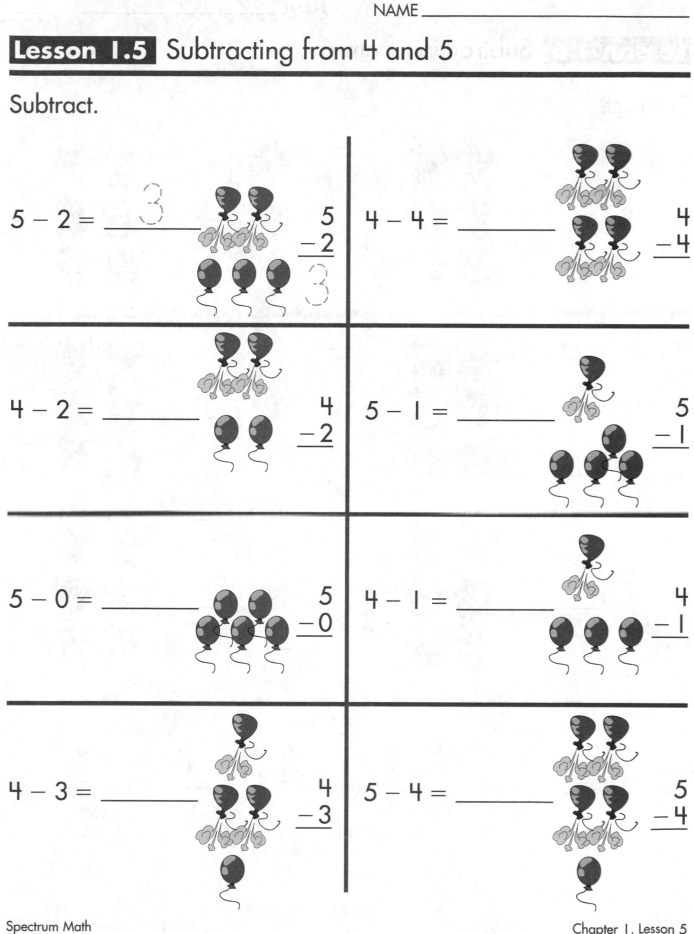

5 − 2 = _____ 3

$$\begin{array}{r} 5 \\ -2 \\ \hline 3 \end{array}$$

4 − 4 = _____

$$\begin{array}{r} 4 \\ -4 \\ \hline \end{array}$$

4 − 2 = _____

$$\begin{array}{r} 4 \\ -2 \\ \hline \end{array}$$

5 − 1 = _____

$$\begin{array}{r} 5 \\ -1 \\ \hline \end{array}$$

5 − 0 = _____

$$\begin{array}{r} 5 \\ -0 \\ \hline \end{array}$$

4 − 1 = _____

$$\begin{array}{r} 4 \\ -1 \\ \hline \end{array}$$

4 − 3 = _____

$$\begin{array}{r} 4 \\ -3 \\ \hline \end{array}$$

5 − 4 = _____

$$\begin{array}{r} 5 \\ -4 \\ \hline \end{array}$$

Lesson 1.6 Subtracting from 6

Subtract.

$6 - 4 = \underline{2}$ $\begin{array}{r} 6 \\ -4 \\ \hline 2 \end{array}$

$6 - 1 = \underline{}$ $\begin{array}{r} 6 \\ -1 \\ \hline \end{array}$

$6 - 0 = \underline{}$ $\begin{array}{r} 6 \\ -0 \\ \hline \end{array}$

$6 - 3 = \underline{}$ $\begin{array}{r} 6 \\ -3 \\ \hline \end{array}$

$6 - 2 = \underline{}$ $\begin{array}{r} 6 \\ -2 \\ \hline \end{array}$

$6 - 5 = \underline{}$ $\begin{array}{r} 6 \\ -5 \\ \hline \end{array}$

$\begin{array}{r} 6 \\ -1 \\ \hline \end{array}$ $\begin{array}{r} 6 \\ -3 \\ \hline \end{array}$ $\begin{array}{r} 6 \\ -2 \\ \hline \end{array}$ $\begin{array}{r} 6 \\ -6 \\ \hline \end{array}$ $\begin{array}{r} 6 \\ -4 \\ \hline \end{array}$ $\begin{array}{r} 6 \\ -5 \\ \hline \end{array}$

Lesson 1.7 Fact Families 0 through 6

Add or subtract.

| 2
+3
5 | 3
+2
5 | 5
−2
3 | 5
−3
2 | 5
+1 | 1
+5 | 6
−5 | 6
−1 |

$3 + 1 = $ _____

$1 + 3 = $ _____

$4 − 3 = $ _____

$4 − 1 = $ _____

$3 + 3 = $ _____

$6 − 3 = $ _____

| 1
+2 | 2
+1 | 3
−1 | 3
−2 | 4
+0 | 0
+4 | 4
−4 | 4
−0 |

| 2
+2 | 4
−2 | 4
+1 | 1
+4 | 5
−4 | 5
−1 |

Lesson 1.7 Fact Families 0 through 6

Add or subtract.

$$2 \atop +4$$ $$4 \atop +2$$ $$6 \atop -2$$ $$6 \atop -4$$ $$1 \atop +1$$ $$2 \atop -1$$

$2 + 0 =$ _____

$0 + 2 =$ _____

$2 - 0 =$ _____

$2 - 2 =$ _____

$5 + 0 =$ _____

$0 + 5 =$ _____

$5 - 5 =$ _____

$5 - 0 =$ _____

$$2 \atop +3$$ $$3 \atop +2$$ $$5 \atop -2$$ $$5 \atop -3$$ $$6 \atop +0$$ $$0 \atop +6$$ $$6 \atop -0$$ $$6 \atop -6$$

$3 + 0 =$ _____

$0 + 3 =$ _____

$3 - 3 =$ _____

$3 - 0 =$ _____

$1 + 0 =$ _____

$0 + 1 =$ _____

$1 - 0 =$ _____

$1 - 1 =$ _____

Lesson 1.8 Problem Solving

SHOW YOUR WORK

Solve each problem.

Tom has 5 🚚.
Maria has 2 🚚.
What is the difference? _____3_____

$$\begin{array}{r} 5 \\ -\ 2 \\ \hline 3 \end{array}$$

There are 3 🍁 on the ground.
1 more 🍁 falls to the ground.
What is 3 + 1? _____

There are 4 🚓.
2 🚓 drive away.
How many are left? _____

Fuji has 2 🧍.
Steve has 1 🧍.
What is the sum? _____

There are 2 🐓.
Then 3 more 🐓 come.
What is 2 plus 3? _____

There are 6 🐦.
1 🐦 flies away.
What is 6 minus 1? _____

Lesson 1.8 Problem Solving

SHOW YOUR WORK

Solve each problem.

Betsy has 5 🌼.
Drew has 1 🌼.
Add 5 plus 1. ___6___

$$\begin{array}{r} 5 \\ + 1 \\ \hline 6 \end{array}$$

Eric saw 2 🏠.
Esther saw 4 🏠.
How many in all? _____

The farmer has 3 🐐.
The farmer gets 3 more 🐐.
How many does the farmer have now? _____

There are 3 🍎.
I ate 1 🍎.
How many are left? _____

There are 5 🦒.
3 🦒 run away.
Subtract 5 − 3. _____

There are 6 ⚾.
I lost 2 ⚾.
How many do I have left? _____

Lesson 1.8 Problem Solving

SHOW YOUR WORK

Solve each problem.

Ella has 1 🎩.
Carlos has 1 🎩.
What is the sum? ___2___

$$\begin{array}{r} 1 \\ + 1 \\ \hline 2 \end{array}$$

I have 1 🤖.
I buy 4 🤖.
What is 1 plus 4? _____

Len has 5 🪙.
Tami has 4 🪙.
What is the difference? _____

There are 4 ✈.
3 ✈ fly away.
Subtract 4 minus 3. _____

Will picked 2 🍑.
Nita picked 2 🍑.
Add 2 + 2. _____

There are 6 ✏.
I took 4 ✏.
How many are left? _____

Lesson 1.9 Adding to 7

Add.

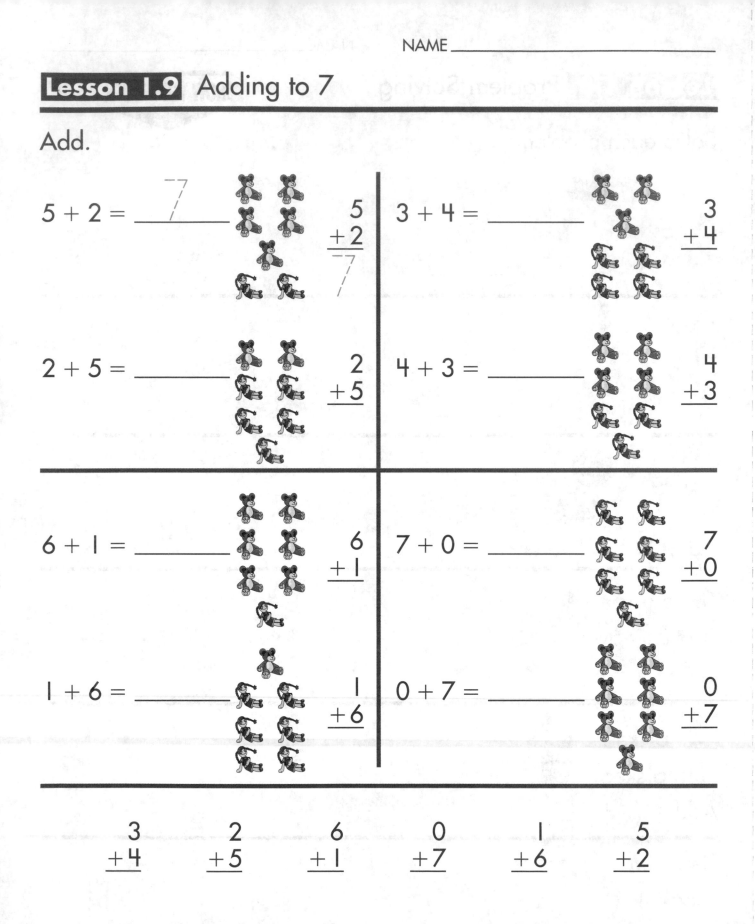

$5 + 2 = \underline{}$

$$\begin{array}{r} 5 \\ +2 \\ \hline 7 \end{array}$$

$3 + 4 = \underline{}$

$$\begin{array}{r} 3 \\ +4 \\ \hline \end{array}$$

$2 + 5 = \underline{}$

$$\begin{array}{r} 2 \\ +5 \\ \hline \end{array}$$

$4 + 3 = \underline{}$

$$\begin{array}{r} 4 \\ +3 \\ \hline \end{array}$$

$6 + 1 = \underline{}$

$$\begin{array}{r} 6 \\ +1 \\ \hline \end{array}$$

$7 + 0 = \underline{}$

$$\begin{array}{r} 7 \\ +0 \\ \hline \end{array}$$

$1 + 6 = \underline{}$

$$\begin{array}{r} 1 \\ +6 \\ \hline \end{array}$$

$0 + 7 = \underline{}$

$$\begin{array}{r} 0 \\ +7 \\ \hline \end{array}$$

$$\begin{array}{r} 3 \\ +4 \\ \hline \end{array} \qquad \begin{array}{r} 2 \\ +5 \\ \hline \end{array} \qquad \begin{array}{r} 6 \\ +1 \\ \hline \end{array} \qquad \begin{array}{r} 0 \\ +7 \\ \hline \end{array} \qquad \begin{array}{r} 1 \\ +6 \\ \hline \end{array} \qquad \begin{array}{r} 5 \\ +2 \\ \hline \end{array}$$

Lesson 1.10 Subtracting from 7

Subtract.

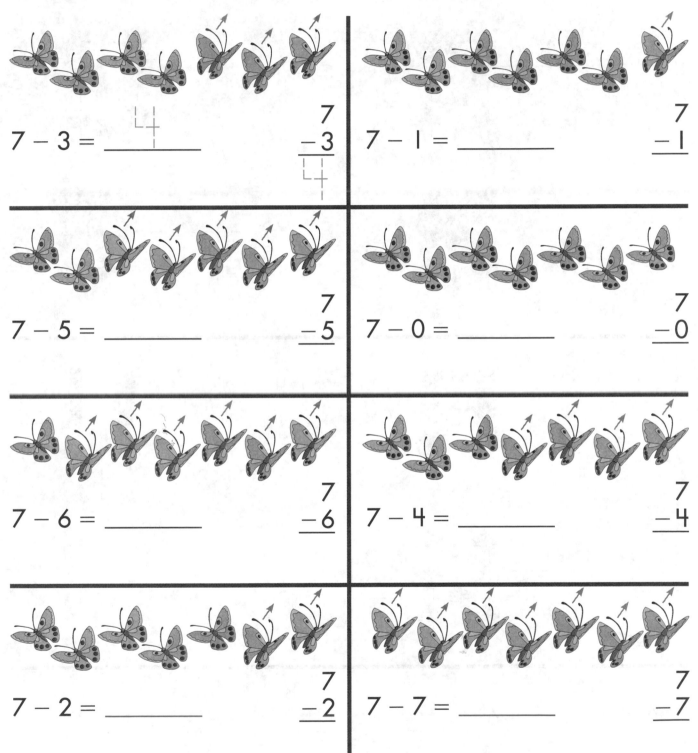

$7 - 3 = \underline{}4$

$\begin{array}{r} 7 \\ -3 \\ \hline 4 \end{array}$

$7 - 1 = \underline{}$

$\begin{array}{r} 7 \\ -1 \\ \hline \end{array}$

$7 - 5 = \underline{}$

$\begin{array}{r} 7 \\ -5 \\ \hline \end{array}$

$7 - 0 = \underline{}$

$\begin{array}{r} 7 \\ -0 \\ \hline \end{array}$

$7 - 6 = \underline{}$

$\begin{array}{r} 7 \\ -6 \\ \hline \end{array}$

$7 - 4 = \underline{}$

$\begin{array}{r} 7 \\ -4 \\ \hline \end{array}$

$7 - 2 = \underline{}$

$\begin{array}{r} 7 \\ -2 \\ \hline \end{array}$

$7 - 7 = \underline{}$

$\begin{array}{r} 7 \\ -7 \\ \hline \end{array}$

Lesson 1.11 Adding to 8

Add.

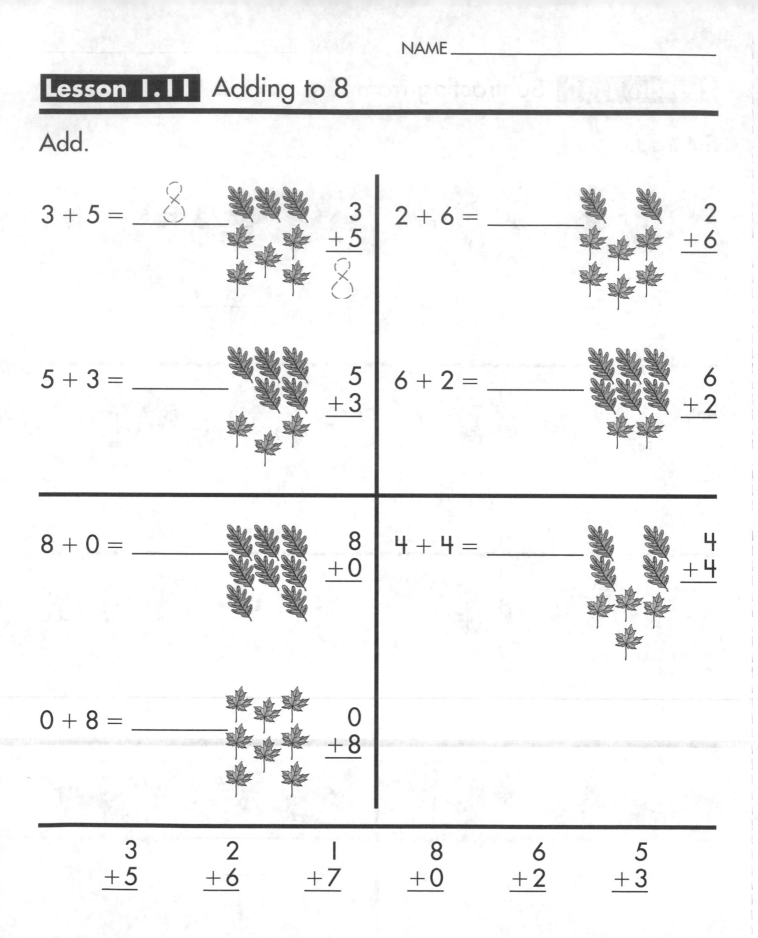

$3 + 5 = \underline{8}$

$\begin{array}{r} 3 \\ +5 \\ \hline 8 \end{array}$

$2 + 6 = \underline{\hspace{2cm}}$

$\begin{array}{r} 2 \\ +6 \\ \hline \end{array}$

$5 + 3 = \underline{\hspace{2cm}}$

$\begin{array}{r} 5 \\ +3 \\ \hline \end{array}$

$6 + 2 = \underline{\hspace{2cm}}$

$\begin{array}{r} 6 \\ +2 \\ \hline \end{array}$

$8 + 0 = \underline{\hspace{2cm}}$

$\begin{array}{r} 8 \\ +0 \\ \hline \end{array}$

$4 + 4 = \underline{\hspace{2cm}}$

$\begin{array}{r} 4 \\ +4 \\ \hline \end{array}$

$0 + 8 = \underline{\hspace{2cm}}$

$\begin{array}{r} 0 \\ +8 \\ \hline \end{array}$

$\begin{array}{r} 3 \\ +5 \\ \hline \end{array}$
$\begin{array}{r} 2 \\ +6 \\ \hline \end{array}$
$\begin{array}{r} 1 \\ +7 \\ \hline \end{array}$
$\begin{array}{r} 8 \\ +0 \\ \hline \end{array}$
$\begin{array}{r} 6 \\ +2 \\ \hline \end{array}$
$\begin{array}{r} 5 \\ +3 \\ \hline \end{array}$

Lesson 1.12 Subtracting from 8

Subtract.

$8 - 2 =$ _____

$\begin{array}{r} 8 \\ -2 \\ \hline \end{array}$

$8 - 4 =$ _____

$\begin{array}{r} 8 \\ -4 \\ \hline \end{array}$

$8 - 6 =$ _____

$\begin{array}{r} 8 \\ -6 \\ \hline \end{array}$

$8 - 7 =$ _____

$\begin{array}{r} 8 \\ -7 \\ \hline \end{array}$

$8 - 1 =$ _____

$\begin{array}{r} 8 \\ -1 \\ \hline \end{array}$

$8 - 8 =$ _____

$\begin{array}{r} 8 \\ -8 \\ \hline \end{array}$

$8 - 3 =$ _____

$\begin{array}{r} 8 \\ -3 \\ \hline \end{array}$

$8 - 5 =$ _____

$\begin{array}{r} 8 \\ -5 \\ \hline \end{array}$

Lesson 1.13 Adding to 9

Add.

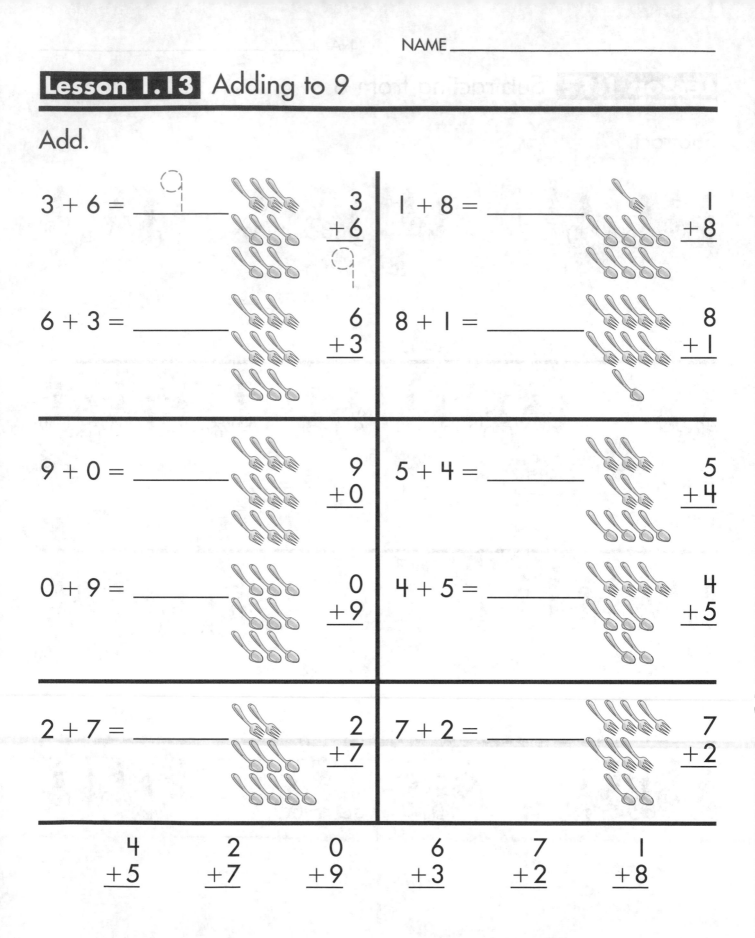

$3 + 6 =$ _____ 9

$$\begin{array}{r} 3 \\ +6 \\ \hline 9 \end{array}$$

$6 + 3 =$ _____

$$\begin{array}{r} 6 \\ +3 \\ \hline \end{array}$$

$1 + 8 =$ _____

$$\begin{array}{r} 1 \\ +8 \\ \hline \end{array}$$

$8 + 1 =$ _____

$$\begin{array}{r} 8 \\ +1 \\ \hline \end{array}$$

$9 + 0 =$ _____

$$\begin{array}{r} 9 \\ +0 \\ \hline \end{array}$$

$0 + 9 =$ _____

$$\begin{array}{r} 0 \\ +9 \\ \hline \end{array}$$

$5 + 4 =$ _____

$$\begin{array}{r} 5 \\ +4 \\ \hline \end{array}$$

$4 + 5 =$ _____

$$\begin{array}{r} 4 \\ +5 \\ \hline \end{array}$$

$2 + 7 =$ _____

$$\begin{array}{r} 2 \\ +7 \\ \hline \end{array}$$

$7 + 2 =$ _____

$$\begin{array}{r} 7 \\ +2 \\ \hline \end{array}$$

$$\begin{array}{r} 4 \\ +5 \\ \hline \end{array} \qquad \begin{array}{r} 2 \\ +7 \\ \hline \end{array} \qquad \begin{array}{r} 0 \\ +9 \\ \hline \end{array} \qquad \begin{array}{r} 6 \\ +3 \\ \hline \end{array} \qquad \begin{array}{r} 7 \\ +2 \\ \hline \end{array} \qquad \begin{array}{r} 1 \\ +8 \\ \hline \end{array}$$

Lesson 1.14 Subtracting from 9

Subtract.

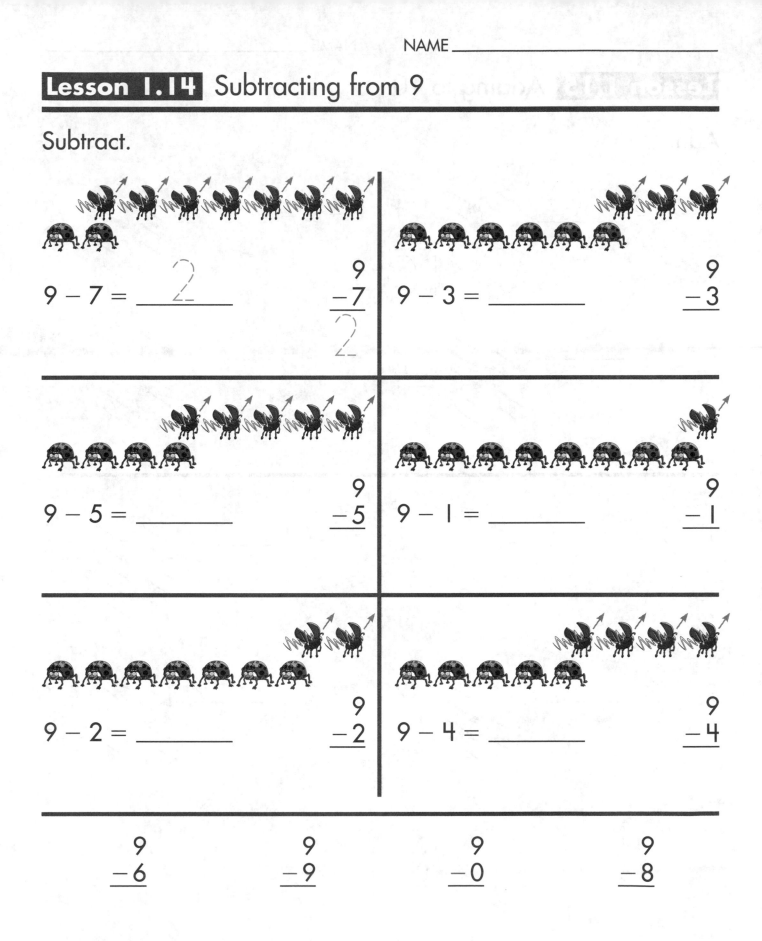

$9 - 7 = \underline{2}$

$\begin{array}{r} 9 \\ -7 \\ \hline 2 \end{array}$

$9 - 3 = \underline{}$

$\begin{array}{r} 9 \\ -3 \\ \hline \end{array}$

$9 - 5 = \underline{}$

$\begin{array}{r} 9 \\ -5 \\ \hline \end{array}$

$9 - 1 = \underline{}$

$\begin{array}{r} 9 \\ -1 \\ \hline \end{array}$

$9 - 2 = \underline{}$

$\begin{array}{r} 9 \\ -2 \\ \hline \end{array}$

$9 - 4 = \underline{}$

$\begin{array}{r} 9 \\ -4 \\ \hline \end{array}$

$\begin{array}{r} 9 \\ -6 \\ \hline \end{array}$

$\begin{array}{r} 9 \\ -9 \\ \hline \end{array}$

$\begin{array}{r} 9 \\ -0 \\ \hline \end{array}$

$\begin{array}{r} 9 \\ -8 \\ \hline \end{array}$

Lesson 1.15 Adding to 10

Add.

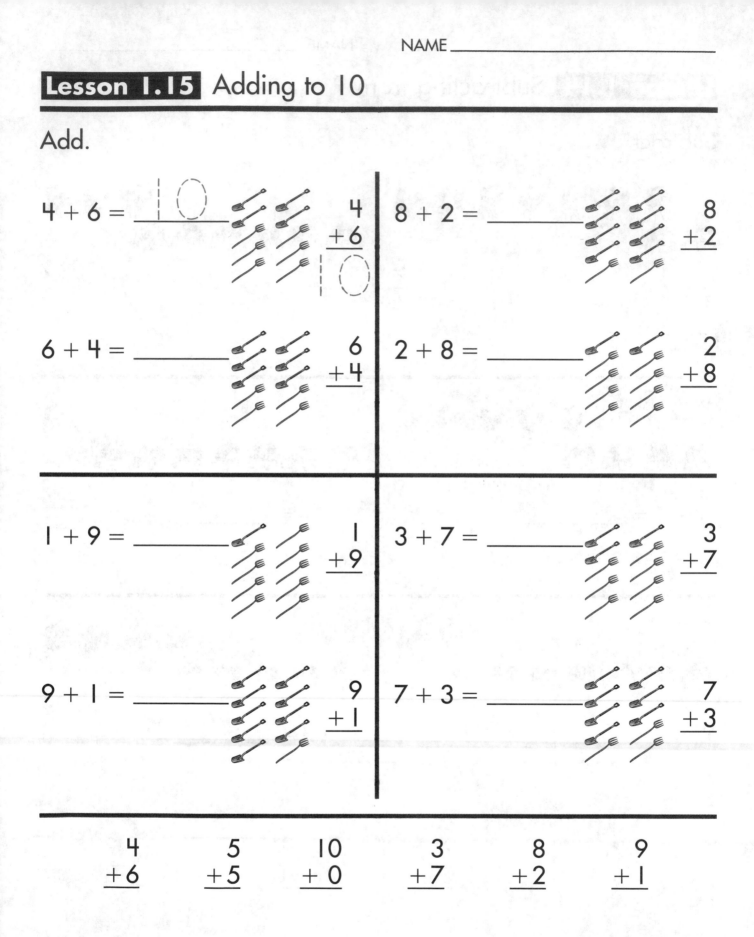

$4 + 6 =$ __10__ $\begin{array}{r} 4 \\ +6 \\ \hline 10 \end{array}$ $8 + 2 =$ _____ $\begin{array}{r} 8 \\ +2 \\ \hline \end{array}$

$6 + 4 =$ _____ $\begin{array}{r} 6 \\ +4 \\ \hline \end{array}$ $2 + 8 =$ _____ $\begin{array}{r} 2 \\ +8 \\ \hline \end{array}$

$1 + 9 =$ _____ $\begin{array}{r} 1 \\ +9 \\ \hline \end{array}$ $3 + 7 =$ _____ $\begin{array}{r} 3 \\ +7 \\ \hline \end{array}$

$9 + 1 =$ _____ $\begin{array}{r} 9 \\ +1 \\ \hline \end{array}$ $7 + 3 =$ _____ $\begin{array}{r} 7 \\ +3 \\ \hline \end{array}$

$\begin{array}{r} 4 \\ +6 \\ \hline \end{array}$ $\begin{array}{r} 5 \\ +5 \\ \hline \end{array}$ $\begin{array}{r} 10 \\ +0 \\ \hline \end{array}$ $\begin{array}{r} 3 \\ +7 \\ \hline \end{array}$ $\begin{array}{r} 8 \\ +2 \\ \hline \end{array}$ $\begin{array}{r} 9 \\ +1 \\ \hline \end{array}$

Lesson 1.16 Subtracting from 10

Subtract.

$10 - 6 = \underline{\quad 4 \quad}$ $\begin{array}{r} 10 \\ - 6 \\ \hline \end{array}$ $\begin{array}{r} 4 \end{array}$

$10 - 5 = \underline{\qquad}$ $\begin{array}{r} 10 \\ - 5 \\ \hline \end{array}$

$10 - 3 = \underline{\qquad}$ $\begin{array}{r} 10 \\ - 3 \\ \hline \end{array}$

$10 - 8 = \underline{\qquad}$ $\begin{array}{r} 10 \\ - 8 \\ \hline \end{array}$

$10 - 1 = \underline{\qquad}$ $\begin{array}{r} 10 \\ - 1 \\ \hline \end{array}$

$10 - 10 = \underline{\qquad}$ $\begin{array}{r} 10 \\ - 10 \\ \hline \end{array}$

$10 - 2 = \underline{\qquad}$ $\begin{array}{r} 10 \\ - 2 \\ \hline \end{array}$

$10 - 9 = \underline{\qquad}$ $\begin{array}{r} 10 \\ - 9 \\ \hline \end{array}$

$10 - 7 = \underline{\qquad}$ $\begin{array}{r} 10 \\ - 7 \\ \hline \end{array}$

$10 - 4 = \underline{\qquad}$ $\begin{array}{r} 10 \\ - 4 \\ \hline \end{array}$

Lesson 1.17 Fact Families 7 through 10

Add or subtract.

4 +5 9	5 +4 9	9 −4 5	9 −5 4

3 +7	7 +3	10 −3	10 −7

5 + 2 = _____

2 + 5 = _____

7 − 5 = _____

7 − 2 = _____

6 + 3 = _____

3 + 6 = _____

9 − 6 = _____

9 − 3 = _____

1 +7	7 +1	8 −1	8 −7

5 +5	10 −5

4 +3	3 +4	7 −4	7 −3

2 +6	6 +2	8 −2	8 −6

Lesson 1.17 Fact Families 7 through 10

Add or subtract.

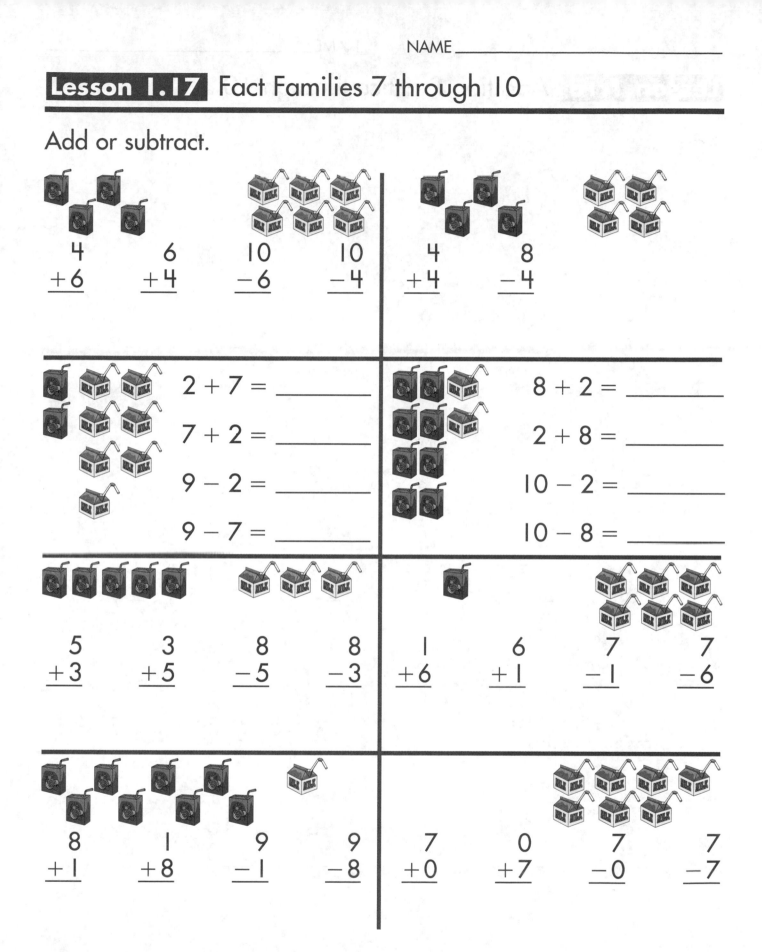

$$
\begin{array}{cc}
4 & 6 \\
+6 & +4 \\
\end{array}
\qquad
\begin{array}{cc}
10 & 10 \\
-6 & -4 \\
\end{array}
\qquad
\begin{array}{cc}
4 & 8 \\
+4 & -4 \\
\end{array}
$$

2 + 7 = _____

7 + 2 = _____

9 − 2 = _____

9 − 7 = _____

8 + 2 = _____

2 + 8 = _____

10 − 2 = _____

10 − 8 = _____

$$
\begin{array}{cccc}
5 & 3 & 8 & 8 \\
+3 & +5 & -5 & -3 \\
\end{array}
\qquad
\begin{array}{cccc}
1 & 6 & 7 & 7 \\
+6 & +1 & -1 & -6 \\
\end{array}
$$

$$
\begin{array}{cccc}
8 & 1 & 9 & 9 \\
+1 & +8 & -1 & -8 \\
\end{array}
\qquad
\begin{array}{cccc}
7 & 0 & 7 & 7 \\
+0 & +7 & -0 & -7 \\
\end{array}
$$

Lesson 1.18 Addition Practice through 10

Add.

3 +5 8	1 +8	7 +2	4 +6	4 +2	2 +5
4 +5	3 +4	9 +1	0 +10	6 +3	3 +7
8 +0	3 +2	0 +7	6 +2	7 +3	0 +9
6 +1	5 +2	8 +2	5 +5	4 +0	2 +7
9 +0	6 +4	1 +6	3 +0	2 +8	5 +3
5 +4	2 +4	7 +0	8 +1	10 + 0	1 +2

Lesson 1.18 Problem Solving

SHOW YOUR WORK

Solve each problem.

There are 8 🛒.
There are 2 🛒.
What is the sum? __10__

$$\begin{array}{r} 8 \\ + 2 \\ \hline 10 \end{array}$$

There are 6 🦛.
3 more 🦛 come.
What is 6 plus 3? _____

I have 4 ✒.
I buy 4 more ✒.
How many do I have now? _____

Ivan has 2 🦕.
Helen has 5 🦕.
What is 2 + 5? _____

There are 7 🐦.
3 more 🐦 come.
How many in all? _____

Lesson 1.19 Subtraction Practice through 10

Subtract.

10 $-\ 4$	9 $-\ 8$	9 $-\ 3$	9 $-\ 5$	10 $-\ 1$	7 $-\ 7$
7 $-\ 5$	8 $-\ 0$	9 $-\ 5$	9 $-\ 6$	7 $-\ 3$	10 -10
10 $-\ 7$	8 $-\ 8$	10 $-\ 5$	6 $-\ 3$	9 $-\ 1$	7 $-\ 0$
8 $-\ 3$	10 $-\ 9$	9 $-\ 9$	8 $-\ 2$	5 $-\ 1$	10 $-\ 0$
9 $-\ 4$	7 $-\ 6$	8 $-\ 1$	10 $-\ 3$	9 $-\ 0$	4 $-\ 2$
10 $-\ 8$	8 $-\ 6$	4 $-\ 1$	9 $-\ 2$	10 $-\ 6$	7 $-\ 4$

Lesson 1.19 Problem Solving

Solve each problem.

There are 7 🐟.

4 🐟 swim away.

How many are left? ___3___

$$\begin{array}{r} 7 \\ -\ 4 \\ \hline 3 \end{array}$$

Brian wants 10 🚗.

He has 3 🚗.

What is the difference? _____

Marla has 8 🍌.

She gives 4 🍌 away.

What is 8 minus 4? _____

There are 7 🎈.

2 🎈 pop.

How many are left? _____

Joan has 9 ✏.

Diego has 5 ✏.

What is the difference? _____

Lesson 1.20 Adding with Money

I penny	I nickel	I dime
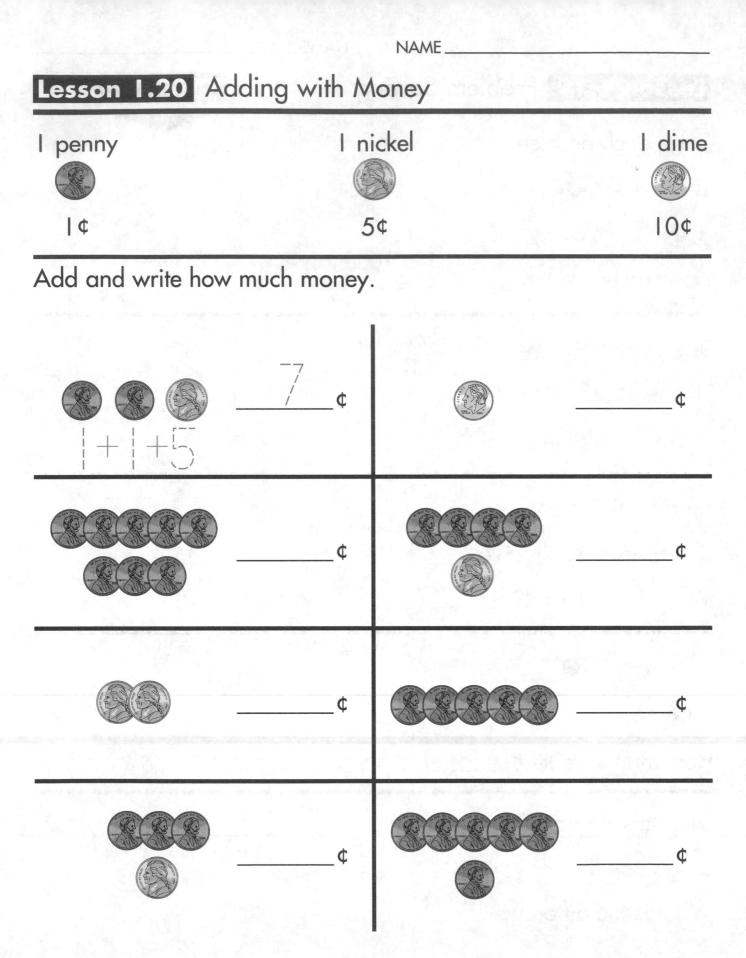		
I¢	5¢	10¢

Add and write how much money.

¯7 ¢

1 + 1 + 5

_____ ¢

_____ ¢   _____ ¢

_____ ¢   _____ ¢

_____ ¢   _____ ¢

Lesson 1.21 Problem Solving

SHOW YOUR WORK

Solve each problem.

John has 10¢.

He buys 🚗 for 3¢.

How much money does he have left? ____7____ ¢

$$\begin{array}{r} 10 \\ -\ 3 \\ \hline 7 \end{array}$$

Ines buys 🎎 for 6¢.

She buys 🐌 for 4¢.

How much money did she spend? _____ ¢

Jordan has 3¢.

He finds 5¢.

How much money does he have? _____ ¢

Elaine has 9¢.

She gives 4¢ to Maxine.

How much money does Elaine have left? _____ ¢

Victor has 7¢.

He buys ✏️ for 6¢.

How much money does he have left? _____ ¢

Lin buys 🍑 for 5¢.

Barb buys 🍎 for 4¢.

How much money did they spend? _____ ¢

Lesson 1.21 Problem Solving

SHOW YOUR WORK

Solve each problem.

David has 10¢.

He buys 🐘 for 7¢.

He has _____ 3 ¢ left.

$$\begin{array}{r} 10¢ \\ -\ 7¢ \\ \hline 3¢ \end{array}$$

Mary buys 🥒 for 3¢.

She buys 🎈 for 5¢.

She spent _____ ¢.

Phil buys 📷 for 6¢.

He buys 🥛 for 4¢.

He spent _____ ¢.

Crystal has 6¢.

Saul has 2¢.

They have _____ ¢.

Rita has 8¢.

She buys 🍎 for 8¢.

She has _____ ¢ left.

Bob has 2¢.

Renee has 5¢.

They have _____ ¢.

Lesson 1.22 More- and Less-Than Facts through 10

SHOW YOUR WORK

Add to find more than. Subtract to find less than.

How many is 2 more than 7 🐿️? _____ 9 $2 + 7 = 9$

What is 1 more than 8 🐕? _____

There are 2 less than 10 🐟.
How many 🐟 are there? _____

What is 1 less than 9 🐷? _____

There is 1 more than 7 🦒.
How many 🦒 are there? _____

What is 2 less than 8 🦁? _____

How many is 1 less than 10 🦆? _____

How many is 1 more than 9 🦋? _____

There is 1 less than 8 🐐.
How many 🐐 are there? _____

Lesson 1.23 Using Addition for Subtraction

Think addition for subtraction. Solve each problem.

8 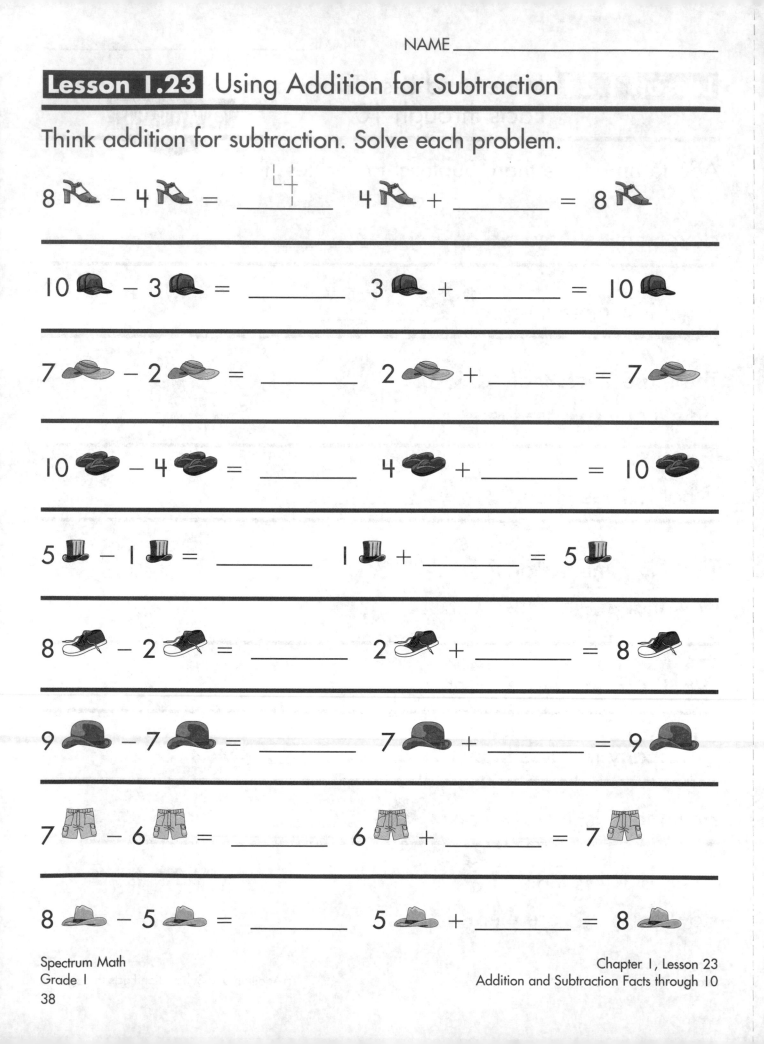 – 4 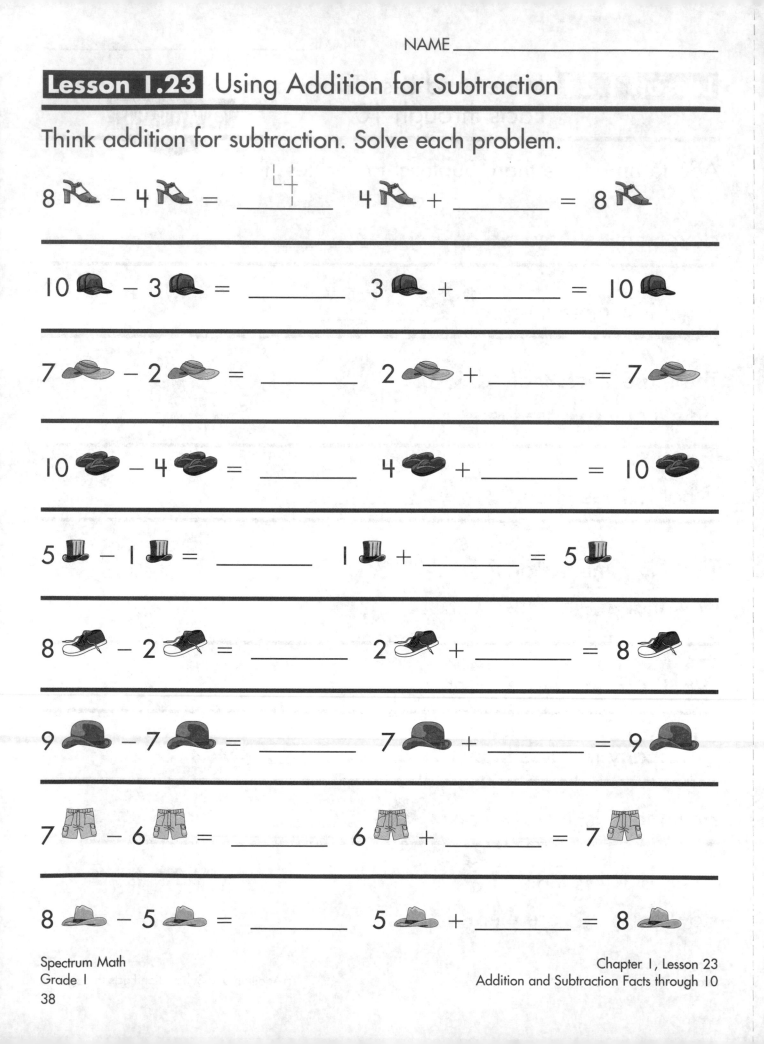 = ___4___   4 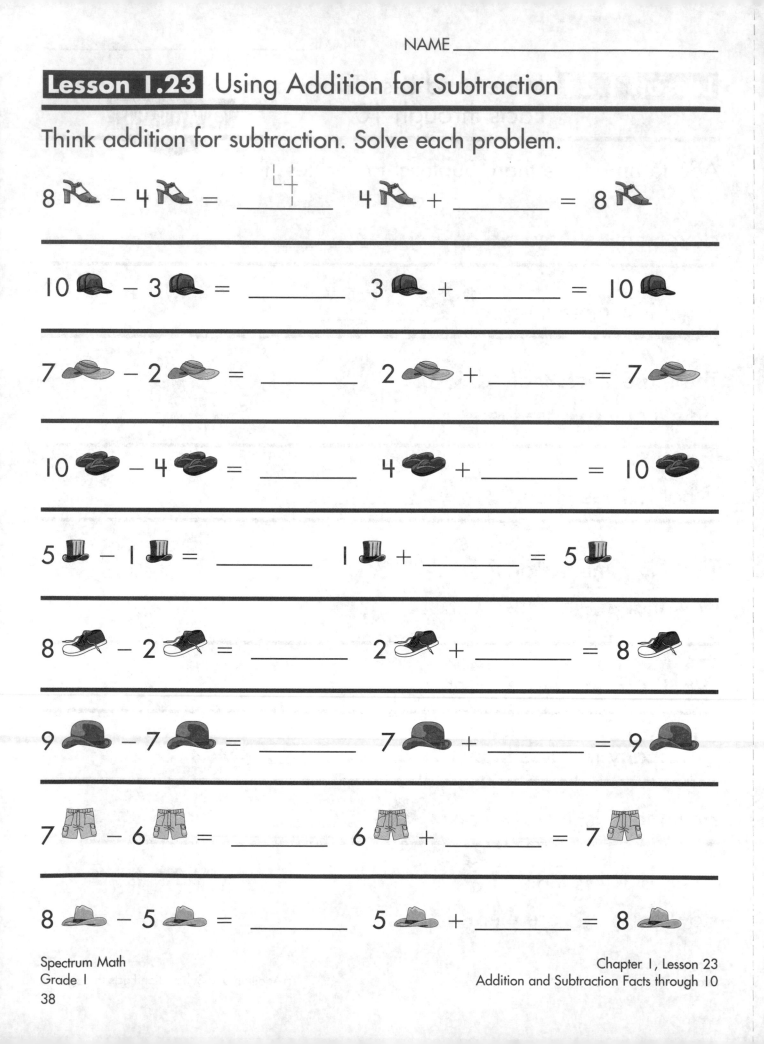 + _____ = 8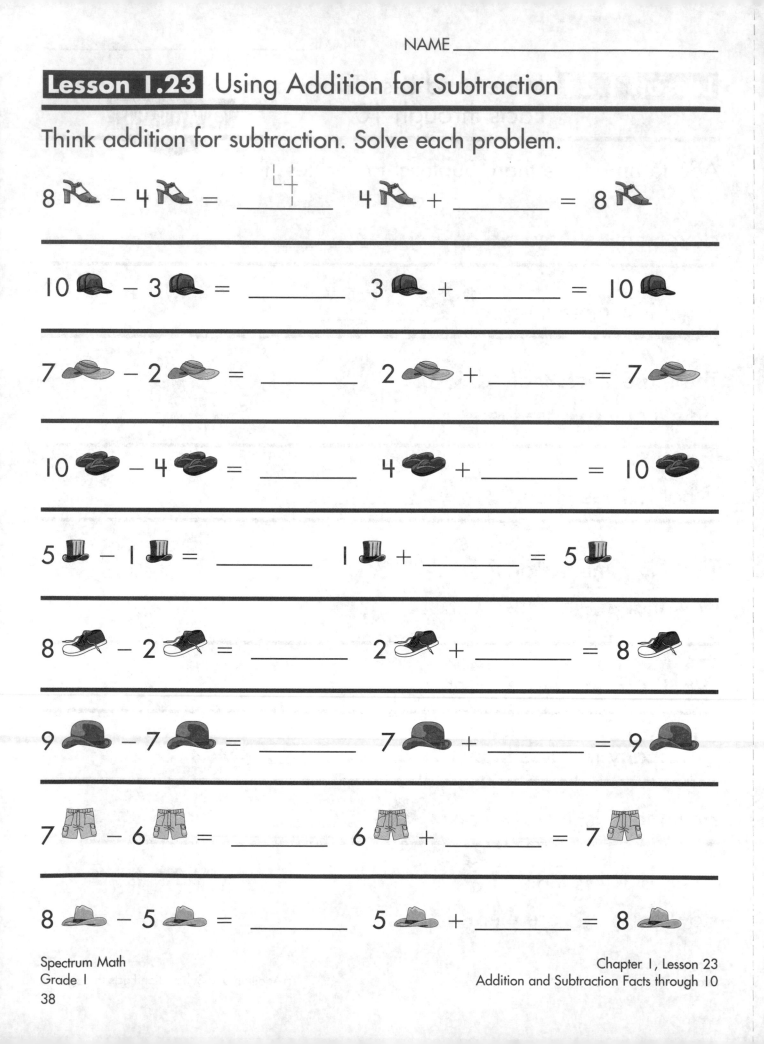

10 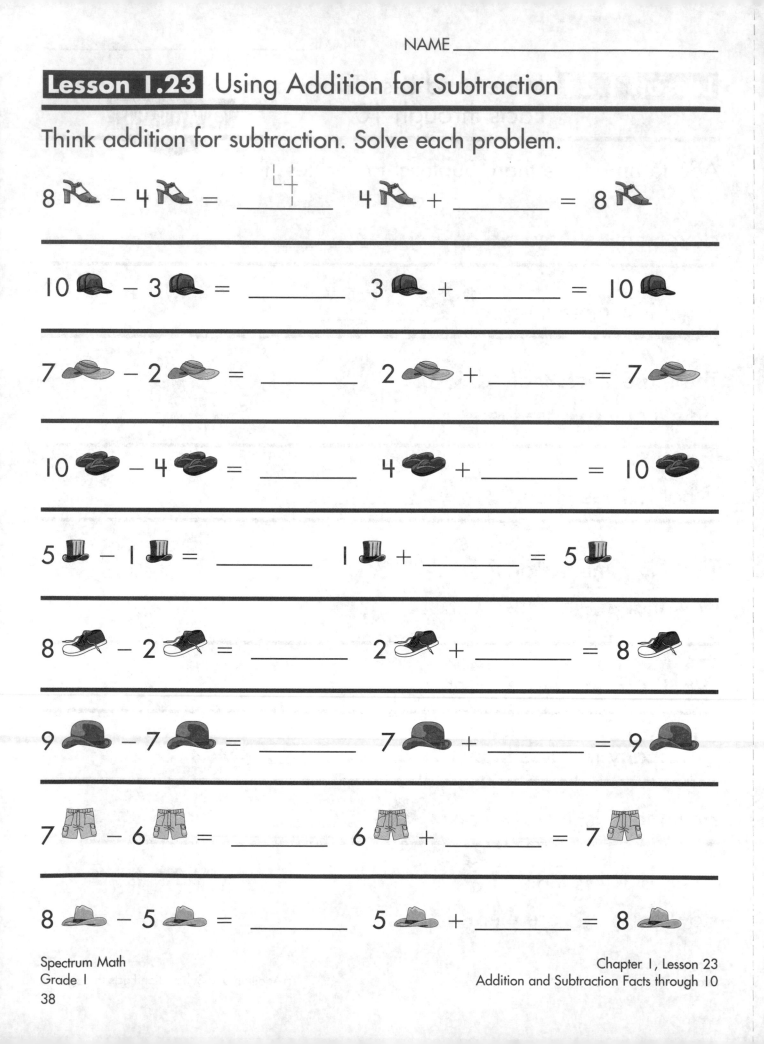 – 3 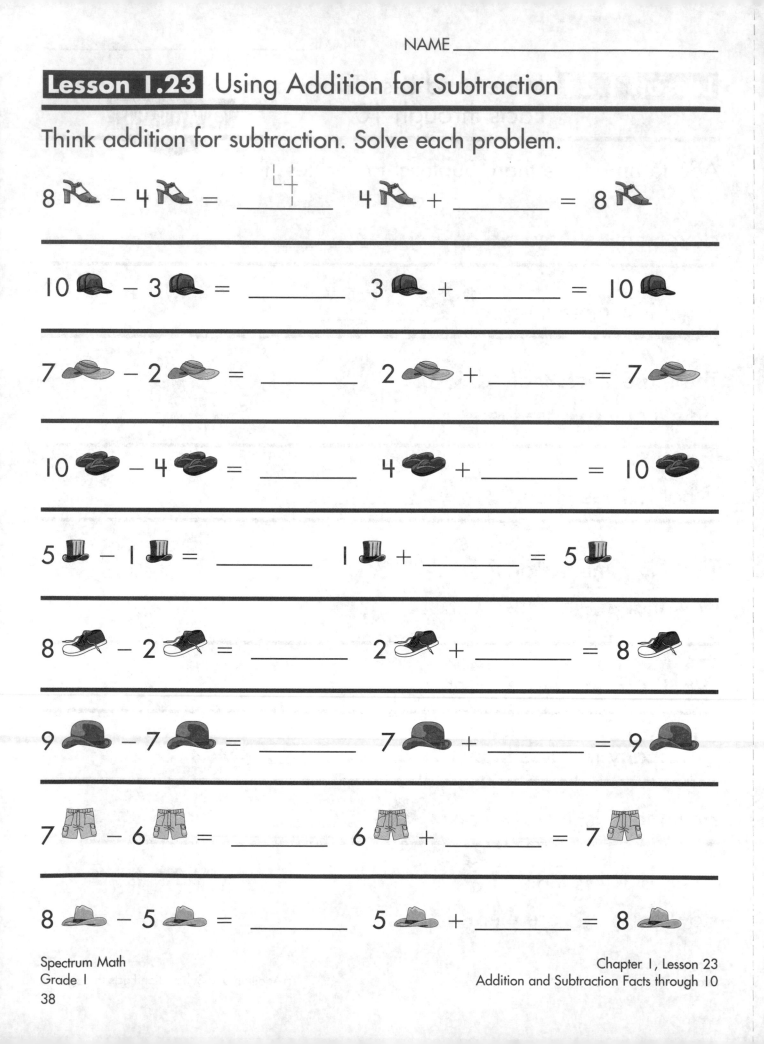 = _____   3 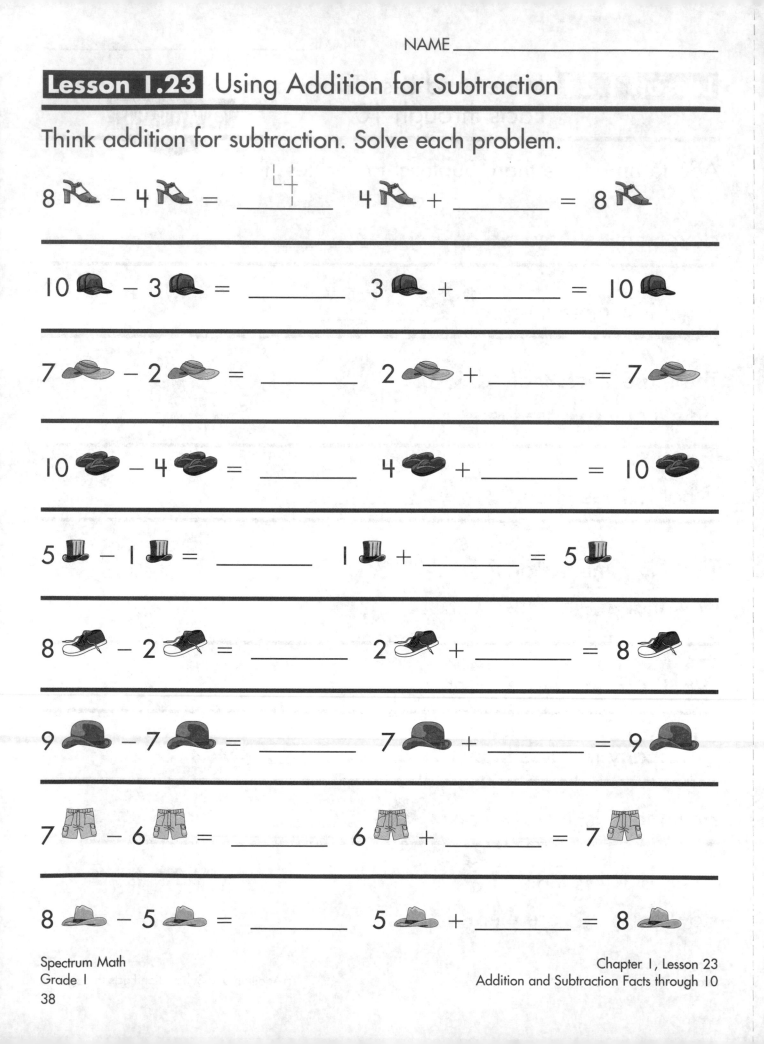 + _____ = 10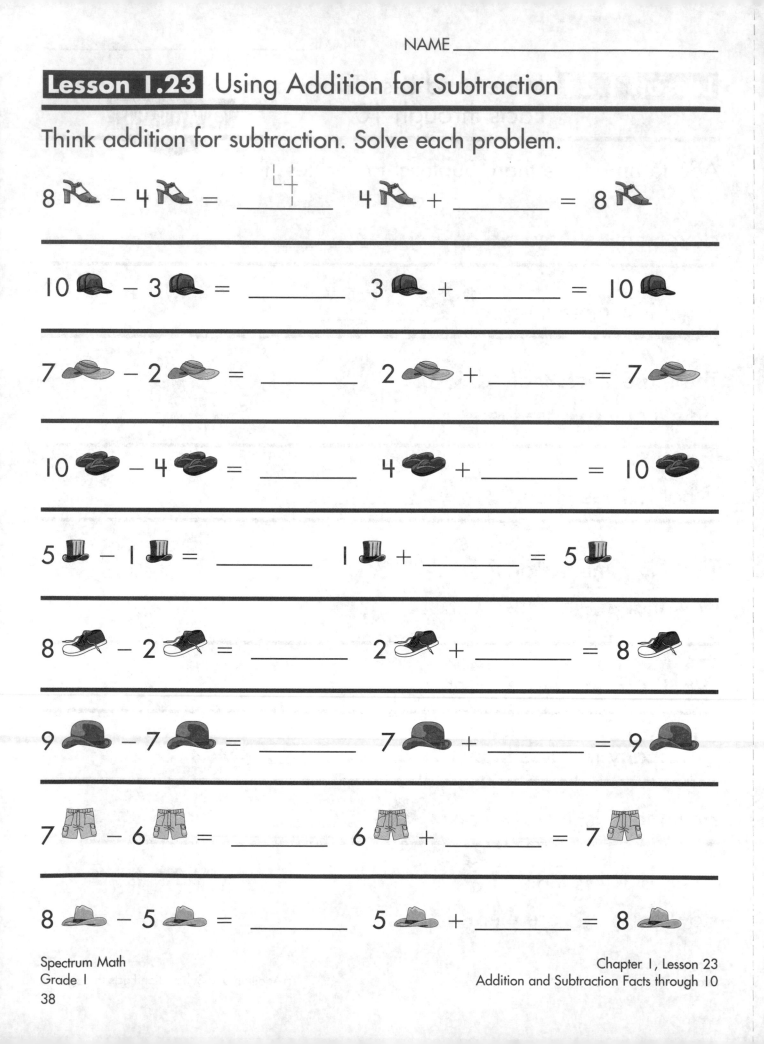

7 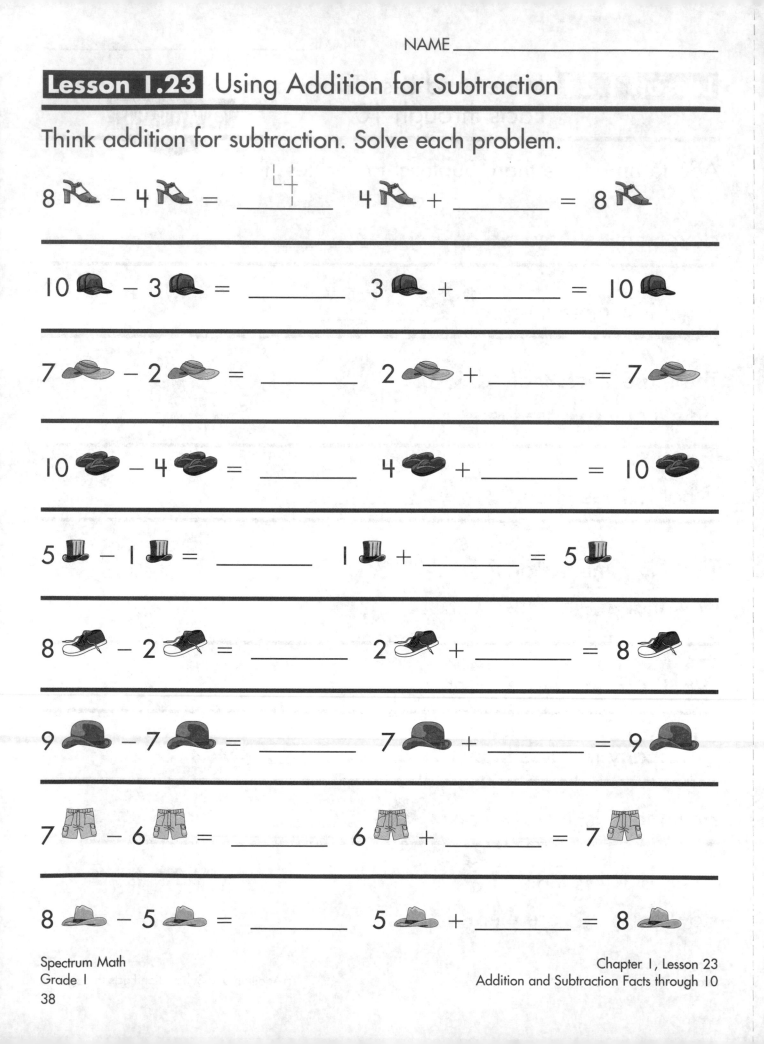 – 2 = _____   2 + _____ = 7

10 – 4 = _____   4 + _____ = 10

5 – 1 = _____   1 + _____ = 5

8 – 2 = _____   2 + _____ = 8

9 – 7 = _____   7 + _____ = 9

7 – 6 = _____   6 + _____ = 7

8 – 5 = _____   5 + _____ = 8

Lesson 1.24 Doubles and Near-Doubles

Add to find the sum.

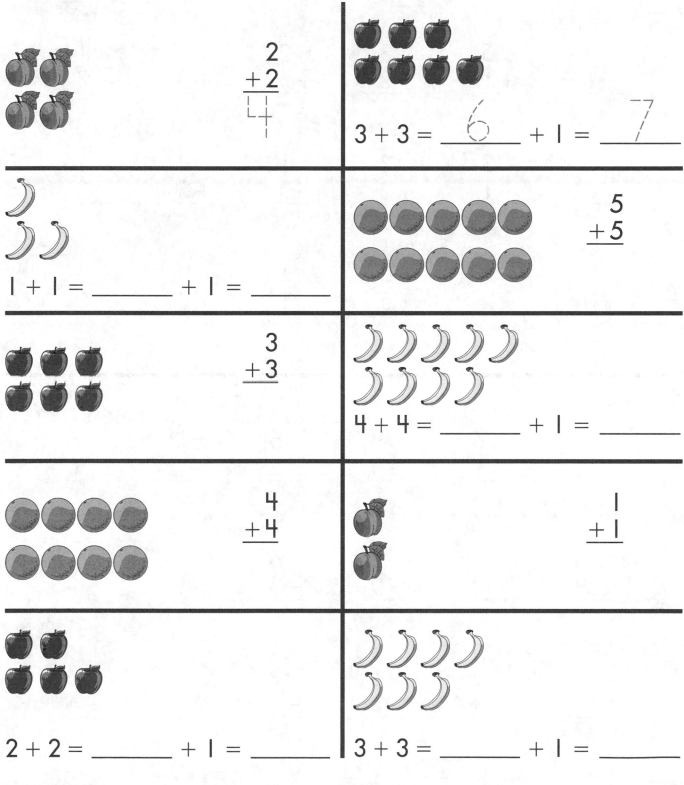

$\begin{array}{r} 2 \\ +2 \\ \hline 4 \end{array}$

$3 + 3 = \underline{6} \quad + 1 = \underline{7}$

$1 + 1 = \underline{} \quad + 1 = \underline{}$

$\begin{array}{r} 5 \\ +5 \\ \hline \end{array}$

$\begin{array}{r} 3 \\ +3 \\ \hline \end{array}$

$4 + 4 = \underline{} \quad + 1 = \underline{}$

$\begin{array}{r} 4 \\ +4 \\ \hline \end{array}$

$\begin{array}{r} 1 \\ +1 \\ \hline \end{array}$

$2 + 2 = \underline{} \quad + 1 = \underline{}$

$3 + 3 = \underline{} \quad + 1 = \underline{}$

Check What You Learned

Addition and Subtraction Facts through 10

Add.

4 +1	5 +1	3 +2	2 +4	3 +0	1 +3
0 +6	3 +1	2 +2	1 +0	3 +3	2 +3
4 +0	1 +2	0 +5	1 +1	4 +2	6 +0

Subtract.

3 −0	6 −1	4 −4	5 −2	3 −2	6 −0
6 −4	5 −3	2 −0	6 −3	5 −5	4 −3
4 −1	5 −4	6 −2	2 −1	5 −1	6 −6

Check What You Learned

SHOW YOUR WORK

Addition and Subtraction Facts through 10

Solve each problem.

There are 2 🦁.
Then 3 more 🦁 come.
Add to find the sum. _____

There are 5 🐦.
2 🐦 fly away.
How many are left? _____

Nate has 4 🎈.
Jane has 1 🎈.
What is the difference? _____

I have 3 🎩.
I buy 3 more 🎩.
What is 3 plus 3? _____

There are 6 🦛.
5 🦛 walk away.
What is 6 minus 5? _____

There are 3 🛶.
Then, 1 more 🛶 comes.
How many in all? _____

Check What You Learned

Addition and Subtraction Facts through 10

Add.

4	0	2	8	5	1
+5	+7	+6	+2	+5	+8

7	1	3	6	8	3
+2	+9	+5	+1	+0	+7

6	4	5	10	7	4
+3	+4	+2	+0	+1	+3

Subtract.

9	10	10	7	8	9
−7	−0	−6	−3	−8	−6

10	9	9	8	8	7
−2	−1	−4	−5	−3	−2

7	9	10	8	10	9
−6	−9	−7	−0	−4	−2

Check What You Learned

SHOW YOUR WORK

Addition and Subtraction Facts through 10

Solve each problem.

There are 8 🐱.
There are 2 🐶.
How many more 🐱 than 🐶 are there? _____

Dan buys 🚚 for 7¢.
He buys 🚓 for 3¢.
How much money did he spend? _____ ¢

There are 9 🍌
Rachel eats 1 🍌.
How many are left? _____

There are 4 🐦.
3 more 🐦 come.
What is the sum? _____

Celia has 10¢.
She buys 🧸 for 8¢.
How much money does she have left? _____ ¢

Jai has 5¢.
He finds 3¢ more.
How much money does he have? _____ ¢

NAME _____

Check What You Know

Place Value

Complete.

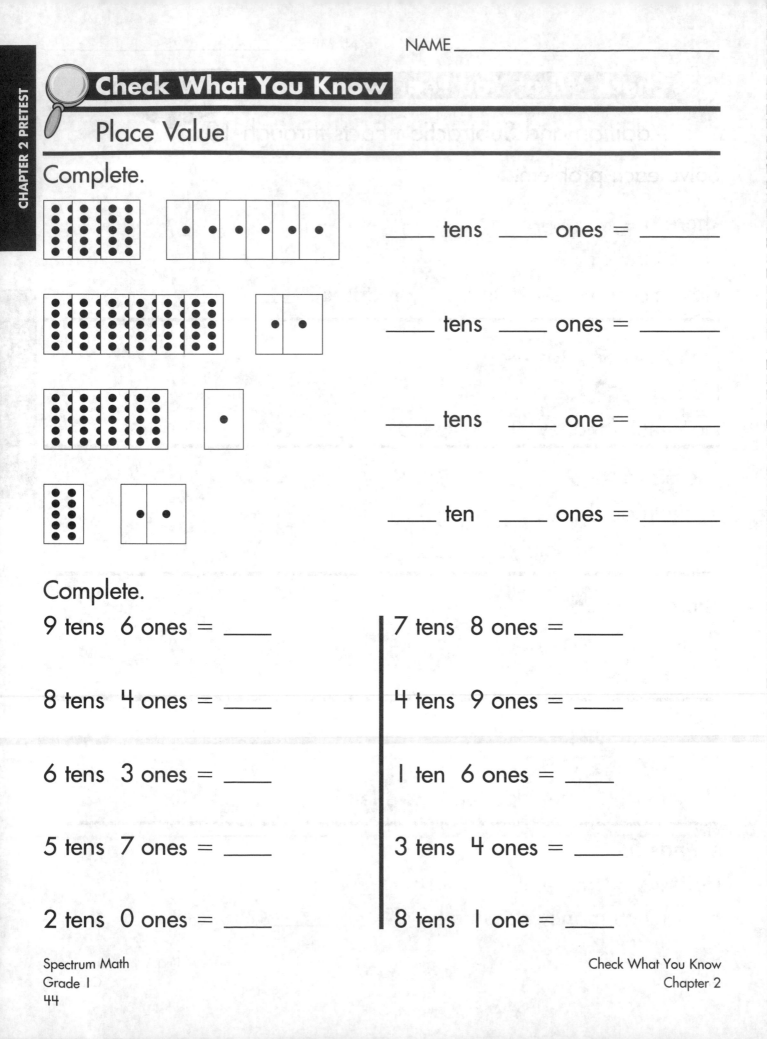

_____ tens _____ ones = _____

_____ tens _____ ones = _____

_____ tens _____ one = _____

_____ ten _____ ones = _____

Complete.

9 tens 6 ones = _____   7 tens 8 ones = _____

8 tens 4 ones = _____   4 tens 9 ones = _____

6 tens 3 ones = _____   1 ten 6 ones = _____

5 tens 7 ones = _____   3 tens 4 ones = _____

2 tens 0 ones = _____   8 tens 1 one = _____

Check What You Know

Place Value

Count forward. Write the missing numbers.

23, 24, _____, 26, 27, _____, 29, _____, _____, 32, 33, 34

72, _____, 74, 75, 76, _____, 78, 79, _____, 81, 82, 83, _____

100, 101, _____, 103, 104, 105, _____, 107, 108, _____, 110

47, 48, 49, _____, _____, _____, 53, 54, _____, 56, 57, 58

112, _____, _____, _____, 116, 117, _____, _____, _____

10, 20, _____, 40, _____, 60, 70, 80, _____, _____, _____, 120

Write > , < , or = to make the following statements true.

40 ☐ 37   77 ☐ 77   18 ☐ 70

55 ☐ 35   38 ☐ 27   9 ☐ 34

22 ☐ 44   85 ☐ 88   71 ☐ 75

14 ☐ 32   30 ☐ 20   65 ☐ 76

59 ☐ 39   43 ☐ 76   29 ☐ 19

52 ☐ 21   36 ☐ 26   64 ☐ 8

Lesson 2.1 Counting and Writing 10 through 14

Complete.

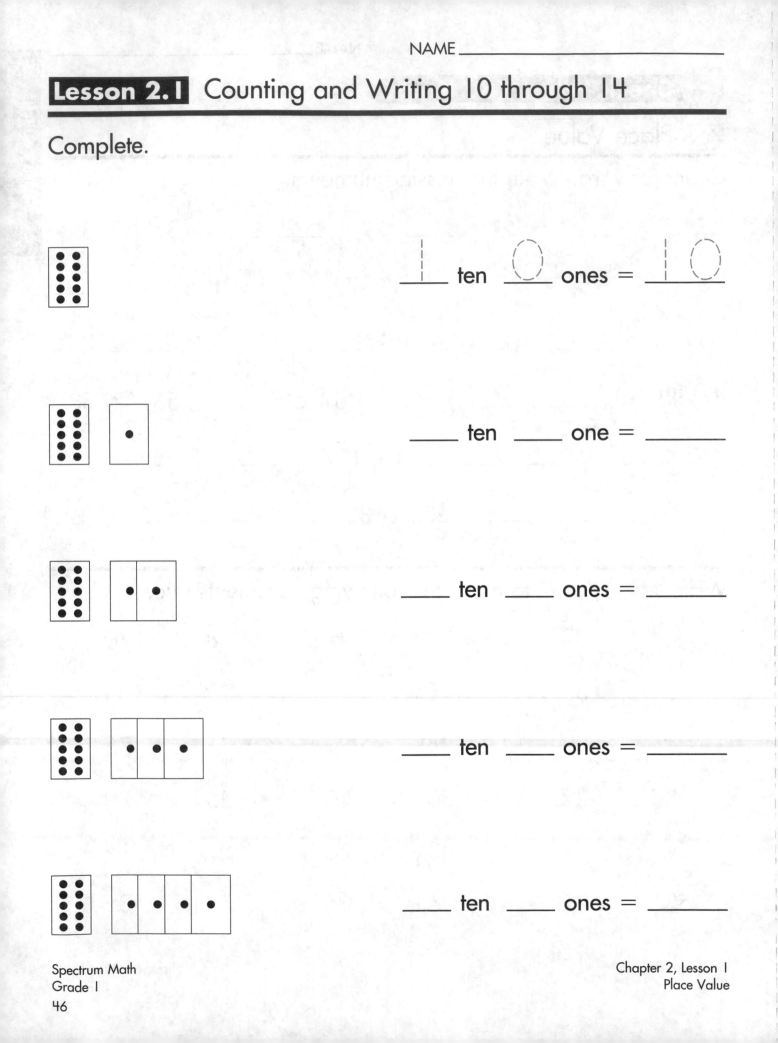

__1__ ten __0__ ones = __10__

___ ten ___ one = _____

___ ten ___ ones = _____

___ ten ___ ones = _____

___ ten ___ ones = _____

Lesson 2.2 Counting and Writing 15 through 19

Complete.

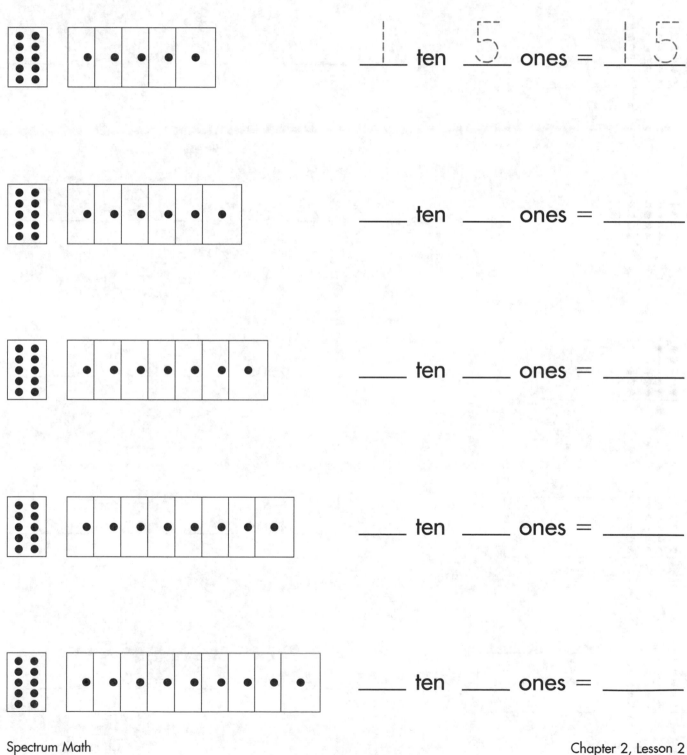

__1__ ten __5__ ones = __15__

___ ten ___ ones = _____

___ ten ___ ones = _____

___ ten ___ ones = _____

___ ten ___ ones = _____

Lesson 2.3 Counting and Writing 20 through 24

Complete.

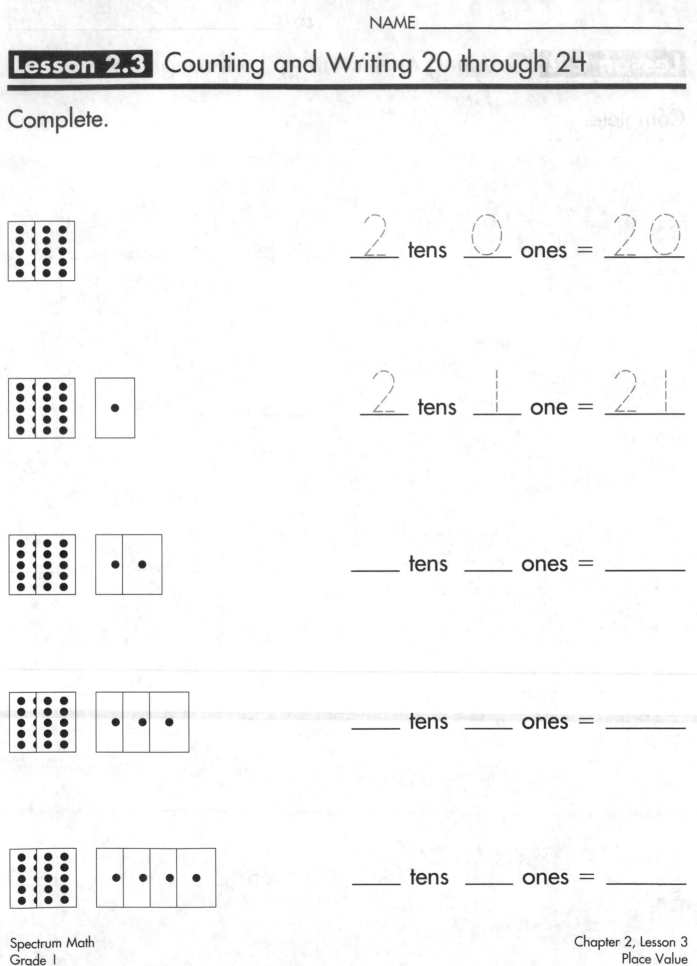

_2_ tens _0_ ones = _20_

_2_ tens _1_ one = _21_

___ tens ___ ones = _____

___ tens ___ ones = _____

___ tens ___ ones = _____

Lesson 2.4 Counting and Writing 25 through 29

Complete.

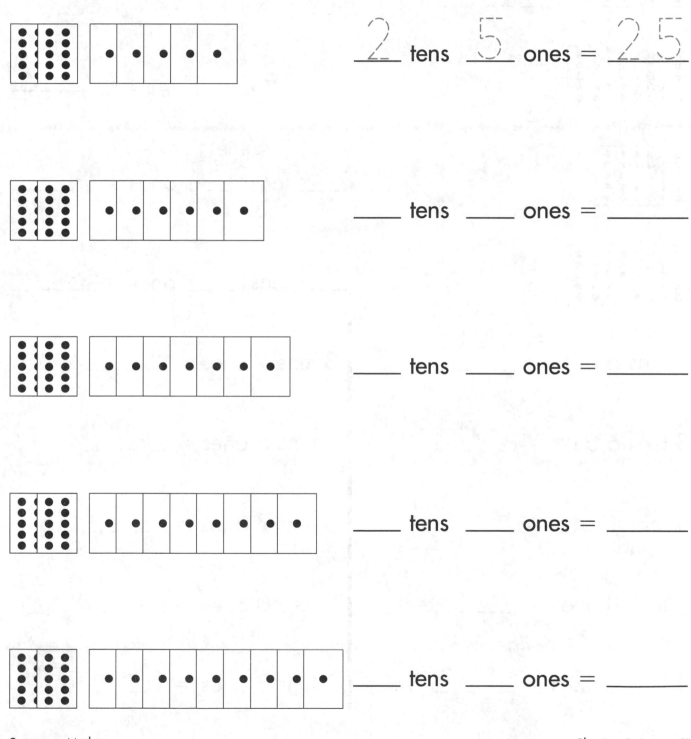

___2___ tens ___5___ ones = ___25___

_____ tens _____ ones = _____

_____ tens _____ ones = _____

_____ tens _____ ones = _____

_____ tens _____ ones = _____

Lesson 2.5 Counting and Writing 30 through 49

Complete.

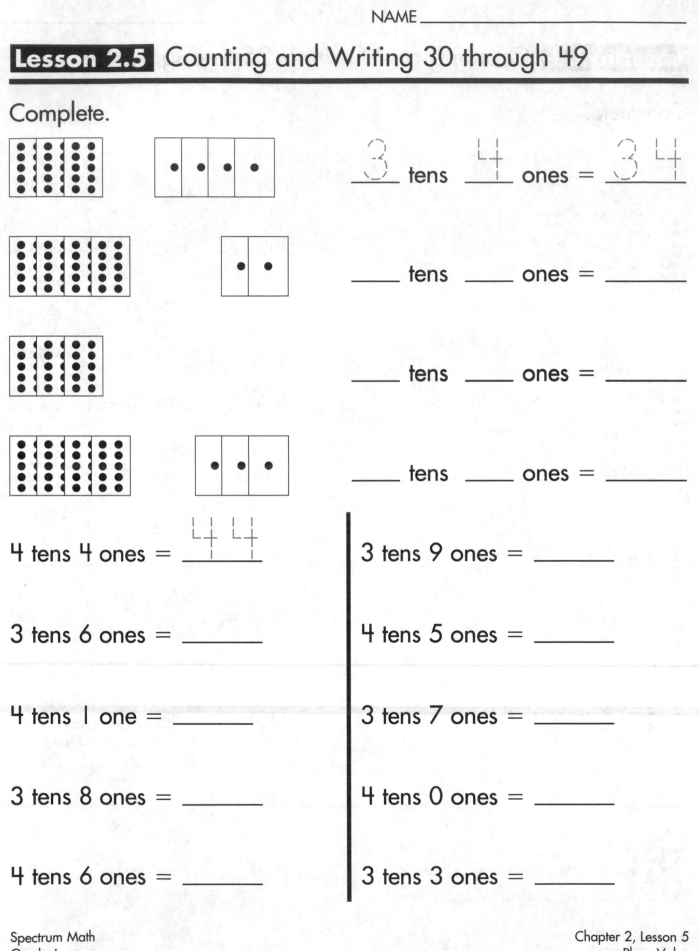

__3__ tens __4__ ones = __34__

____ tens ____ ones = _____

____ tens ____ ones = _____

____ tens ____ ones = _____

4 tens 4 ones = __44__

3 tens 9 ones = _____

3 tens 6 ones = _____

4 tens 5 ones = _____

4 tens 1 one = _____

3 tens 7 ones = _____

3 tens 8 ones = _____

4 tens 0 ones = _____

4 tens 6 ones = _____

3 tens 3 ones = _____

Lesson 2.6 Counting and Writing 50 through 69

Complete.

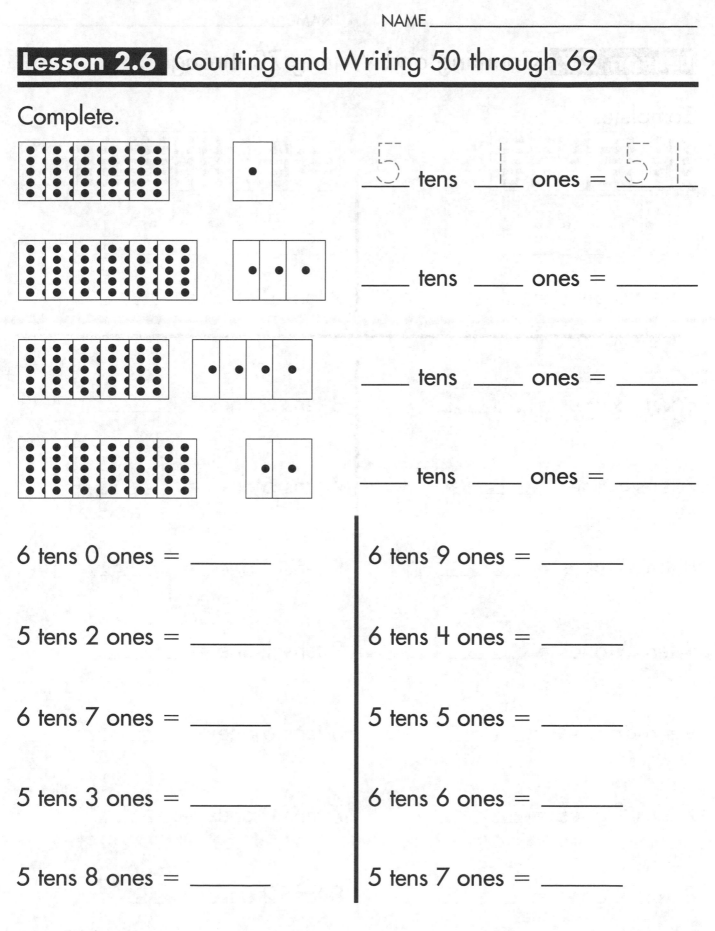

__5__ tens __1__ ones = __51__

_____ tens _____ ones = _____

_____ tens _____ ones = _____

_____ tens _____ ones = _____

6 tens 0 ones = _____   6 tens 9 ones = _____

5 tens 2 ones = _____   6 tens 4 ones = _____

6 tens 7 ones = _____   5 tens 5 ones = _____

5 tens 3 ones = _____   6 tens 6 ones = _____

5 tens 8 ones = _____   5 tens 7 ones = _____

Lesson 2.7 Counting and Writing 70 through 99

Complete.

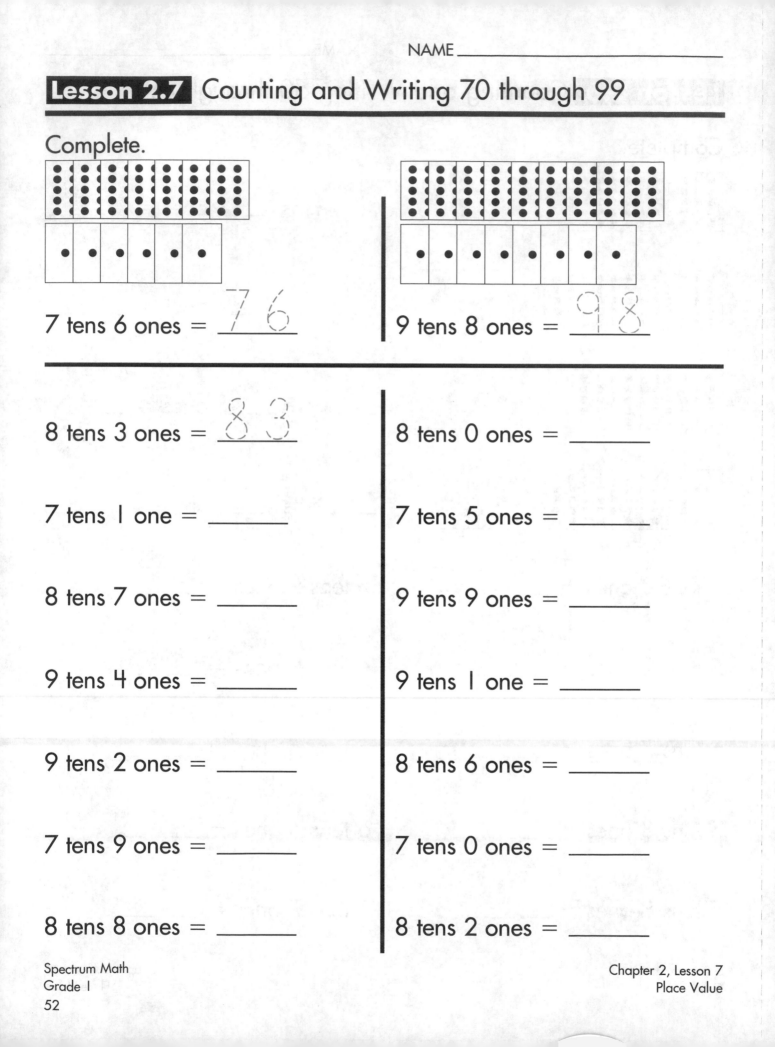

7 tens 6 ones = 76

9 tens 8 ones = 98

8 tens 3 ones = 83

8 tens 0 ones = _____

7 tens 1 one = _____

7 tens 5 ones = _____

8 tens 7 ones = _____

9 tens 9 ones = _____

9 tens 4 ones = _____

9 tens 1 one = _____

9 tens 2 ones = _____

8 tens 6 ones = _____

7 tens 9 ones = _____

7 tens 0 ones = _____

8 tens 8 ones = _____

8 tens 2 ones = _____

Lesson 2.8 Counting to 120

Count forward. Write the missing numbers.

1		3				7			10
11			14		16		18		
	22			25			28		30
	32			35		37			40
		43		45				49	
51				55		57			60
61			64		66		68		
		73					78		
81				85					90
			94		96		98		
		103							
	112			115		117		119	

Lesson 2.9 Counting Forward and Backward to 120

Count forward. Write the missing numbers.

36, 37, _38_, 39, _40_, 41, 42, _43_, 44, 45, _46_

92, 93, ___, 95, 96, ___, 98, 99, ___, ___, 102, 103

___, 67, 68, ___, 70, 71, ___, 73, 74, 75, ___, 77

100, 101, ___, 103, 104, ___, 106, ___, 108, 109, ___, 111

___, 10, 15, ___, 25, 30, 35, ___, 45, 50, 55, ___

___, 20, 30, ___, 50, ___, 70, 80, ___, ___, ___, ___

Count backward. Write the missing numbers.

79, ___, 77, 76, ___, 74, 73, 72, ___, 70, 69, ___

84, ___, 82, 81, ___, 79, 78, 77, ___, ___, 74, 73

24, 22, ___, 18, 16, ___, 12, ___, 8, 6, ___, 2

120, ___, 110, 105, ___, 95, 90, ___, ___, 75, 70, 65

75, 70, ___, 60, 55, ___, 45, 40, 35, ___, 25, ___

___, ___, 90, ___, 70, 60, ___, ___, 30, ___

Lesson 2.10 Comparing Numbers

Compare 2-digit numbers.

53 $>$ 36   Compare tens. 5 is greater than 3. 53 is greater than 36.

73 $<$ 76   If tens are the same, compare ones. 3 is less than 6. 73 is less than 76.

Compare 2-digit numbers. Use > (greater than), < (less than), or = (equal to).

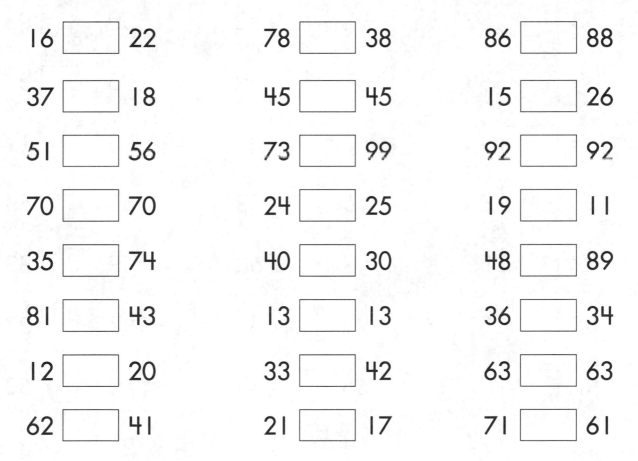

16 ☐ 22   78 ☐ 38   86 ☐ 88

37 ☐ 18   45 ☐ 45   15 ☐ 26

51 ☐ 56   73 ☐ 99   92 ☐ 92

70 ☐ 70   24 ☐ 25   19 ☐ 11

35 ☐ 74   40 ☐ 30   48 ☐ 89

81 ☐ 43   13 ☐ 13   36 ☐ 34

12 ☐ 20   33 ☐ 42   63 ☐ 63

62 ☐ 41   21 ☐ 17   71 ☐ 61

Lesson 2.10 Comparing Numbers

Compare 2-digit numbers. Use > (greater than), < (less than), or = (equal to).

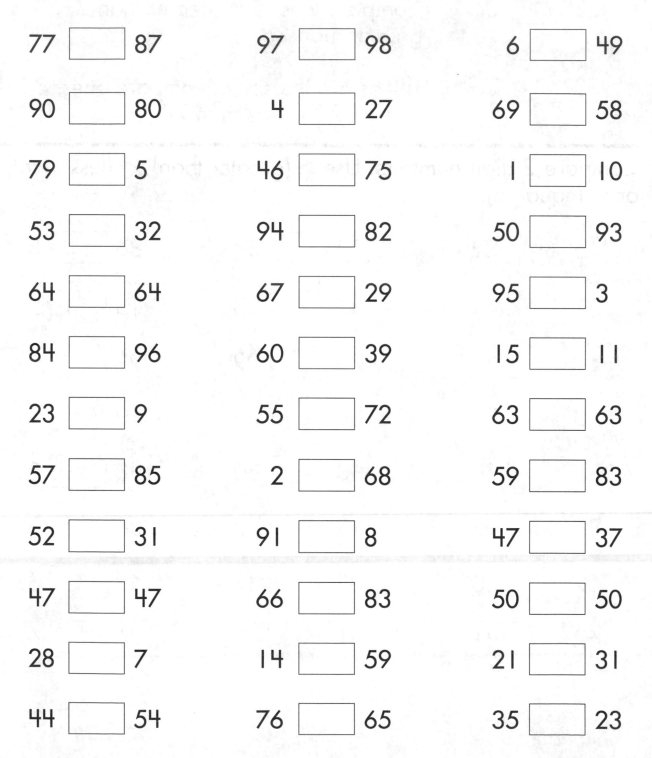

77	☐	87	97	☐	98	6	☐	49

77 ☐ 87   97 ☐ 98   6 ☐ 49

90 ☐ 80   4 ☐ 27   69 ☐ 58

79 ☐ 5   46 ☐ 75   1 ☐ 10

53 ☐ 32   94 ☐ 82   50 ☐ 93

64 ☐ 64   67 ☐ 29   95 ☐ 3

84 ☐ 96   60 ☐ 39   15 ☐ 11

23 ☐ 9   55 ☐ 72   63 ☐ 63

57 ☐ 85   2 ☐ 68   59 ☐ 83

52 ☐ 31   91 ☐ 8   47 ☐ 37

47 ☐ 47   66 ☐ 83   50 ☐ 50

28 ☐ 7   14 ☐ 59   21 ☐ 31

44 ☐ 54   76 ☐ 65   35 ☐ 23

Check What You Learned

Place Value

Complete.

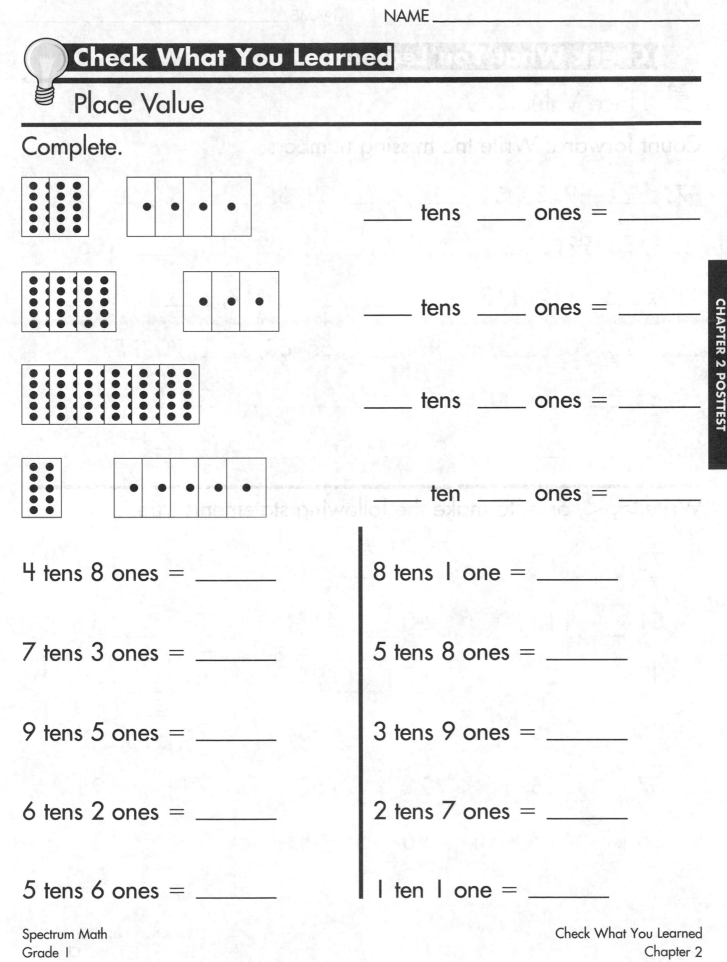

_____ tens _____ ones = _____

_____ tens _____ ones = _____

_____ tens _____ ones = _____

_____ ten _____ ones = _____

4 tens 8 ones = _____   8 tens 1 one = _____

7 tens 3 ones = _____   5 tens 8 ones = _____

9 tens 5 ones = _____   3 tens 9 ones = _____

6 tens 2 ones = _____   2 tens 7 ones = _____

5 tens 6 ones = _____   1 ten 1 one = _____

Check What You Learned

Place Value

Count forward. Write the missing numbers.

47, ____, 49, 50, 51, ____, ____, 54, 55, ____, 57, 58

____, 96, 97, ____, ____, 100, ____, 102, 103, ____, 105

110, ____, 112, 113, ____, ____, ____, 117, ____, 119, ____

____, 25, 30, ____, 40, 45, ____, 55, 60, ____, 70, 75

60, 65, ____, 75, 80, 85, ____, ____, ____, 105, 110, ____, ____

40, ____, ____, ____, 80, 90, 100, ____, 120

Write >, <, or = to make the following statements true.

73 ☐ 60   61 ☐ 51   16 ☐ 68

81 ☐ 13   90 ☐ 17   54 ☐ 5

44 ☐ 33   67 ☐ 95   41 ☐ 69

45 ☐ 45   93 ☐ 93   78 ☐ 79

57 ☐ 56   72 ☐ 62   74 ☐ 25

86 ☐ 97   46 ☐ 48   84 ☐ 3

Mid-Test Chapters 1–2

Add or subtract.

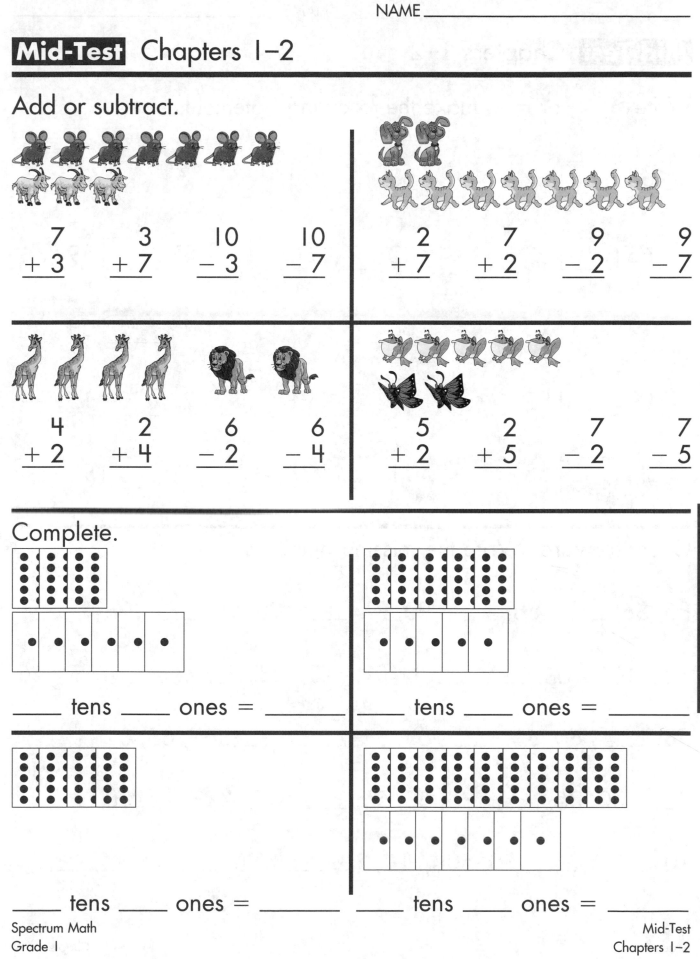

7 + 3	3 + 7	10 − 3	10 − 7

2 + 7	7 + 2	9 − 2	9 − 7

4 + 2	2 + 4	6 − 2	6 − 4

5 + 2	2 + 5	7 − 2	7 − 5

Complete.

____ tens ____ ones = _____

____ tens ____ ones = _____

____ tens ____ ones = _____

____ tens ____ ones = _____

Mid-Test Chapters 1–2

Write >, <, or = to make the following statements true.

66 ☐ 49   58 ☐ 58   6 ☐ 68

63 ☐ 53   42 ☐ 50   87 ☐ 89

12 ☐ 25   68 ☐ 54   24 ☐ 54

92 ☐ 82   10 ☐ 91   23 ☐ 15

28 ☐ 58   11 ☐ 31   98 ☐ 94

Count forward. Write the missing numbers.

85, 86, ____, 88, ____, 90, 91, ____, 93, 94, ____, 96

104, 105, 106, ____, ____, 109, 110, 111, ____, ____, 114, 115

58, ____, 60, 61, ____, 63, 64, ____, ____, 67, 68, 69

____, 30, 35, ____, 45, 50, 55, ____, 65, 70, ____, 80

10, ____, ____, 40, 50, ____, 70, ____, 90, ____, ____, ____

Mid-Test Chapters 1–2

Add.

5 +4	3 +2	8 +1	4 +4	0 +9	2 +8
6 +3	7 +0	9 +1	2 +3	1 +5	0 +4
4 +6	2 +7	6 +0	1 +6	0 +8	4 +1
1 +0	3 +3	5 +2	8 +2	5 +3	6 +1
7 +3	2 +4	3 +5	0 +5	1 +7	0 +2
0 +0	2 +1	4 +2	5 +0	1 +3	0 +7
2 +6	8 +0	6 +4	4 +5	3 +6	7 +3

Mid-Test Chapters 1–2

Subtract.

8 − 6	5 − 4	9 − 1	10 − 7	2 − 0	4 − 2
6 − 3	7 − 6	9 − 5	4 − 4	3 − 1	1 − 0
8 − 2	10 − 8	9 − 9	6 − 5	8 − 4	9 − 3
10 − 4	9 − 6	5 − 2	7 − 4	8 − 8	10 − 3
6 − 1	3 − 3	10 − 2	8 − 0	6 − 4	10 − 1
9 − 7	8 − 5	10 −10	5 − 3	1 − 1	5 − 0
8 − 3	10 − 0	9 − 2	10 − 6	3 − 2	2 − 2

CHAPTERS 1–2 MID-TEST

NAME _____

SHOW YOUR WORK

Solve each problem.

I have 4¢.

I find 5¢.

How much money do I have? _____ ¢

There are 6 🐱.

2 more 🐱 come.

What is the sum of 6 plus 2? _____

Jerome has 3 🚗.

Carla has 3 🚗.

How many in all? _____

Paula buys 🍪 for 2¢.

She buys 🍌 for 3¢.

How much money did she spend? _____ ¢

Andy buys 🧃 for 7¢.

He buys 🥜 for 3¢.

How much money did he spend? _____ ¢

There is 1 🦒.

4 more 🦒 come.

What is 1 + 4? _____

Mid-Test Chapters 1-2

SHOW YOUR WORK

Solve each problem.

Brooke has 5¢.

She buys _____ for 1¢.

How much money does she have left? _____ ¢

There are 7 🦋.

5 🦋 fly away.

How many 🦋 are left? _____

Drew wants 9 🌭.

He has 4 🌭.

How many more 🌭 does he want? _____

Mike has 10¢.

Eva has 8¢.

How much more money does Mike have? _____ ¢

There are 8 🐕.

2 🐕 run away.

What is 8 minus 2? _____

Toshi has 4¢.

She buys 🧃 for 3¢.

How much money does she have left? _____ ¢

CHAPTERS 1-2 MID-TEST

Check What You Know

Addition and Subtraction Facts through 20

Add.

5 +6	9 +9	8 +7	6 +8	4 +9	7 +5
8 +9	8 +8	7 +9	8 +5	6 +6	7 +4
9 +6	7 +6	7 +7	11 +8	12 +7	11 +9

Subtract.

15 − 7	13 − 9	17 − 8	18 − 7	12 − 6	11 − 4
19 − 7	13 − 6	18 − 9	15 − 6	16 − 8	14 − 8
12 − 9	14 − 6	17 − 9	16 − 9	20 − 8	11 − 5

Check What You Know

SHOW YOUR WORK

Addition and Subtraction Facts through 20

Solve each problem.

There are 8 ⬤ in a jar.

There are 9 ⬤ on the table.

How many ⬤ in all? _____

There are 12 🐟.

5 🐟 swim away.

How many 🐟 are left? _____

There are 20 ⚾ on the shelf.

9 ⚾ roll off.

How many ⚾ are still on the shelf? _____

There are 6 👡.

There are 8 👟.

How many shoes in all? _____

I have 15 👕.

8 👕 are dirty.

How many 👕 are clean? _____

Lesson 3.1 Adding to 11

Add.

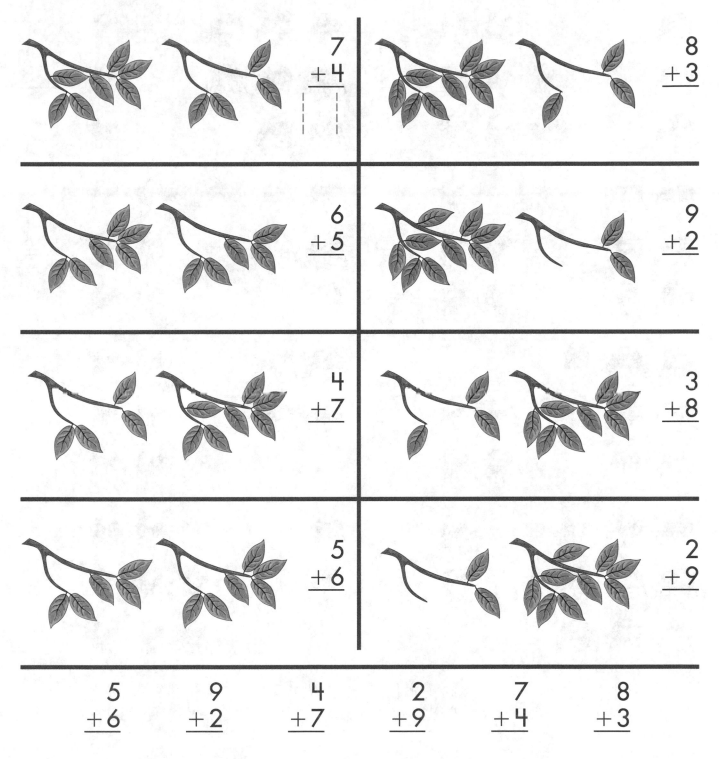

$$\begin{array}{r} 7 \\ +4 \\ \hline \end{array}$$

$$\begin{array}{r} 8 \\ +3 \\ \hline \end{array}$$

$$\begin{array}{r} 6 \\ +5 \\ \hline \end{array}$$

$$\begin{array}{r} 9 \\ +2 \\ \hline \end{array}$$

$$\begin{array}{r} 4 \\ +7 \\ \hline \end{array}$$

$$\begin{array}{r} 3 \\ +8 \\ \hline \end{array}$$

$$\begin{array}{r} 5 \\ +6 \\ \hline \end{array}$$

$$\begin{array}{r} 2 \\ +9 \\ \hline \end{array}$$

$$\begin{array}{r} 5 \\ +6 \\ \hline \end{array} \qquad \begin{array}{r} 9 \\ +2 \\ \hline \end{array} \qquad \begin{array}{r} 4 \\ +7 \\ \hline \end{array} \qquad \begin{array}{r} 2 \\ +9 \\ \hline \end{array} \qquad \begin{array}{r} 7 \\ +4 \\ \hline \end{array} \qquad \begin{array}{r} 8 \\ +3 \\ \hline \end{array}$$

Lesson 3.2 Subtracting from 11

Subtract.

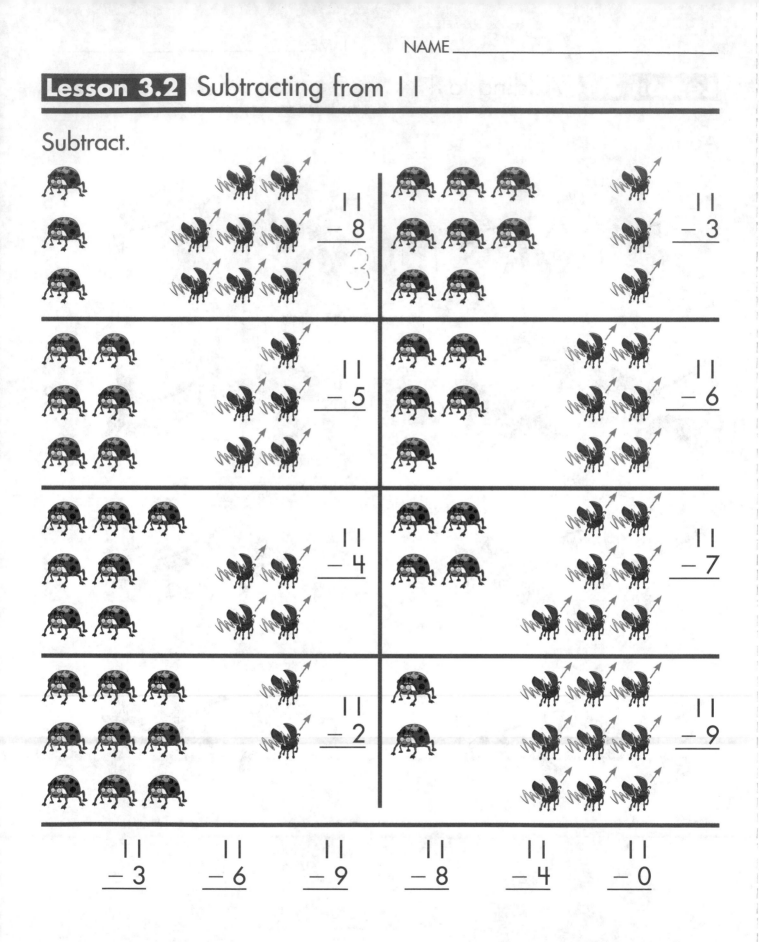

$$\begin{array}{r} 11 \\ -\ 8 \\ \hline \end{array}$$

$$\begin{array}{r} 11 \\ -\ 3 \\ \hline \end{array}$$

$$\begin{array}{r} 11 \\ -\ 5 \\ \hline \end{array}$$

$$\begin{array}{r} 11 \\ -\ 6 \\ \hline \end{array}$$

$$\begin{array}{r} 11 \\ -\ 4 \\ \hline \end{array}$$

$$\begin{array}{r} 11 \\ -\ 7 \\ \hline \end{array}$$

$$\begin{array}{r} 11 \\ -\ 2 \\ \hline \end{array}$$

$$\begin{array}{r} 11 \\ -\ 9 \\ \hline \end{array}$$

$$\begin{array}{r} 11 \\ -\ 3 \\ \hline \end{array}$$
$$\begin{array}{r} 11 \\ -\ 6 \\ \hline \end{array}$$
$$\begin{array}{r} 11 \\ -\ 9 \\ \hline \end{array}$$
$$\begin{array}{r} 11 \\ -\ 8 \\ \hline \end{array}$$
$$\begin{array}{r} 11 \\ -\ 4 \\ \hline \end{array}$$
$$\begin{array}{r} 11 \\ -\ 0 \\ \hline \end{array}$$

Lesson 3.3 Adding to 12

Add.

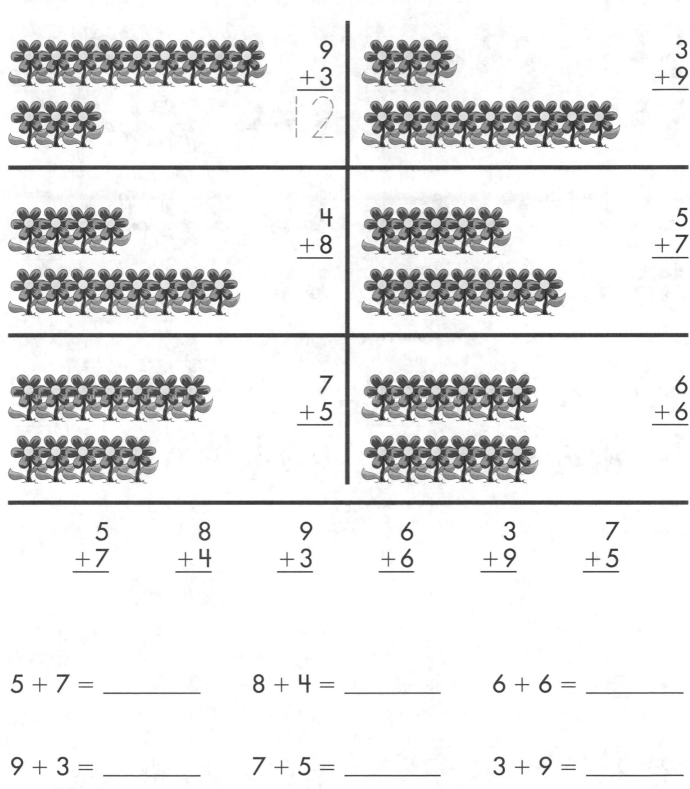

	9		3
	+3		+9
	12		

| | 4 | | 5 |
| | +8 | | +7 |

| | 7 | | 6 |
| | +5 | | +6 |

5	8	9	6	3	7
+7	+4	+3	+6	+9	+5

5 + 7 = _____   8 + 4 = _____   6 + 6 = _____

9 + 3 = _____   7 + 5 = _____   3 + 9 = _____

Lesson 3.4 Subtracting from 12

Subtract.

$\begin{array}{r} 12 \\ -\ 7 \\ \hline 5 \end{array}$

$\begin{array}{r} 12 \\ -\ 5 \\ \hline \end{array}$

$\begin{array}{r} 12 \\ -\ 6 \\ \hline \end{array}$

$\begin{array}{r} 12 \\ -\ 8 \\ \hline \end{array}$

$\begin{array}{r} 12 \\ -\ 9 \\ \hline \end{array}$

$\begin{array}{r} 12 \\ -\ 3 \\ \hline \end{array}$

$\begin{array}{r} 12 \\ -\ 4 \\ \hline \end{array}$
$\begin{array}{r} 12 \\ -\ 3 \\ \hline \end{array}$
$\begin{array}{r} 12 \\ -\ 8 \\ \hline \end{array}$
$\begin{array}{r} 12 \\ -\ 7 \\ \hline \end{array}$
$\begin{array}{r} 12 \\ -\ 6 \\ \hline \end{array}$
$\begin{array}{r} 12 \\ -\ 5 \\ \hline \end{array}$

$12 - 9 = $ _____ $12 - 8 = $ _____ $12 - 6 = $ _____

$12 - 7 = $ _____ $12 - 3 = $ _____ $12 - 4 = $ _____

Lesson 3.5 Adding to 13

Add.

$$\begin{array}{r} 6 \\ +7 \\ \hline 13 \end{array}$$

$$\begin{array}{r} 7 \\ +6 \\ \hline \end{array}$$

$$\begin{array}{r} 4 \\ +9 \\ \hline \end{array}$$

$$\begin{array}{r} 9 \\ +4 \\ \hline \end{array}$$

$$\begin{array}{r} 8 \\ +5 \\ \hline \end{array}$$

$$\begin{array}{r} 5 \\ +8 \\ \hline \end{array}$$

$$\begin{array}{r} 7 \\ +6 \\ \hline \end{array}$$
$$\begin{array}{r} 5 \\ +8 \\ \hline \end{array}$$
$$\begin{array}{r} 9 \\ +4 \\ \hline \end{array}$$
$$\begin{array}{r} 6 \\ +7 \\ \hline \end{array}$$
$$\begin{array}{r} 4 \\ +9 \\ \hline \end{array}$$
$$\begin{array}{r} 8 \\ +5 \\ \hline \end{array}$$

$5 + 8 = $ _____ $4 + 9 = $ _____ $7 + 6 = $ _____

$9 + 4 = $ _____ $8 + 5 = $ _____ $6 + 7 = $ _____

Lesson 3.6 Subtracting from 13

Subtract.

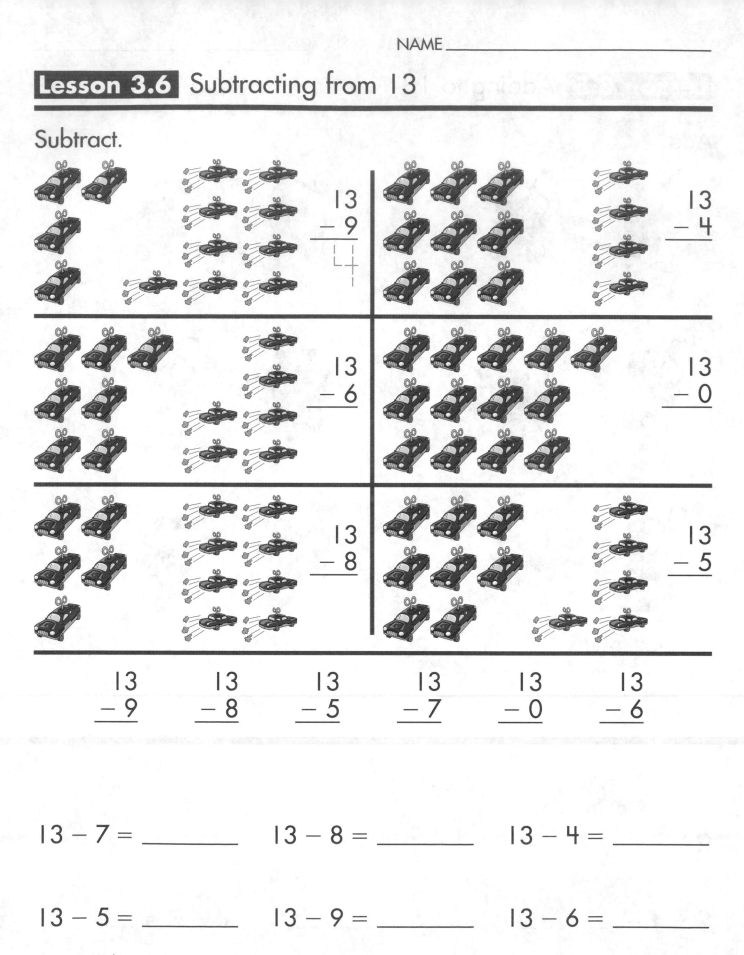

$$\begin{array}{r} 13 \\ -\ 9 \\ \hline 4 \end{array}$$

$$\begin{array}{r} 13 \\ -\ 4 \\ \hline \end{array}$$

$$\begin{array}{r} 13 \\ -\ 6 \\ \hline \end{array}$$

$$\begin{array}{r} 13 \\ -\ 0 \\ \hline \end{array}$$

$$\begin{array}{r} 13 \\ -\ 8 \\ \hline \end{array}$$

$$\begin{array}{r} 13 \\ -\ 5 \\ \hline \end{array}$$

$$\begin{array}{r} 13 \\ -\ 9 \\ \hline \end{array} \qquad \begin{array}{r} 13 \\ -\ 8 \\ \hline \end{array} \qquad \begin{array}{r} 13 \\ -\ 5 \\ \hline \end{array} \qquad \begin{array}{r} 13 \\ -\ 7 \\ \hline \end{array} \qquad \begin{array}{r} 13 \\ -\ 0 \\ \hline \end{array} \qquad \begin{array}{r} 13 \\ -\ 6 \\ \hline \end{array}$$

$13 - 7 =$ _____ $13 - 8 =$ _____ $13 - 4 =$ _____

$13 - 5 =$ _____ $13 - 9 =$ _____ $13 - 6 =$ _____

Lesson 3.7 Adding to 14

Add.

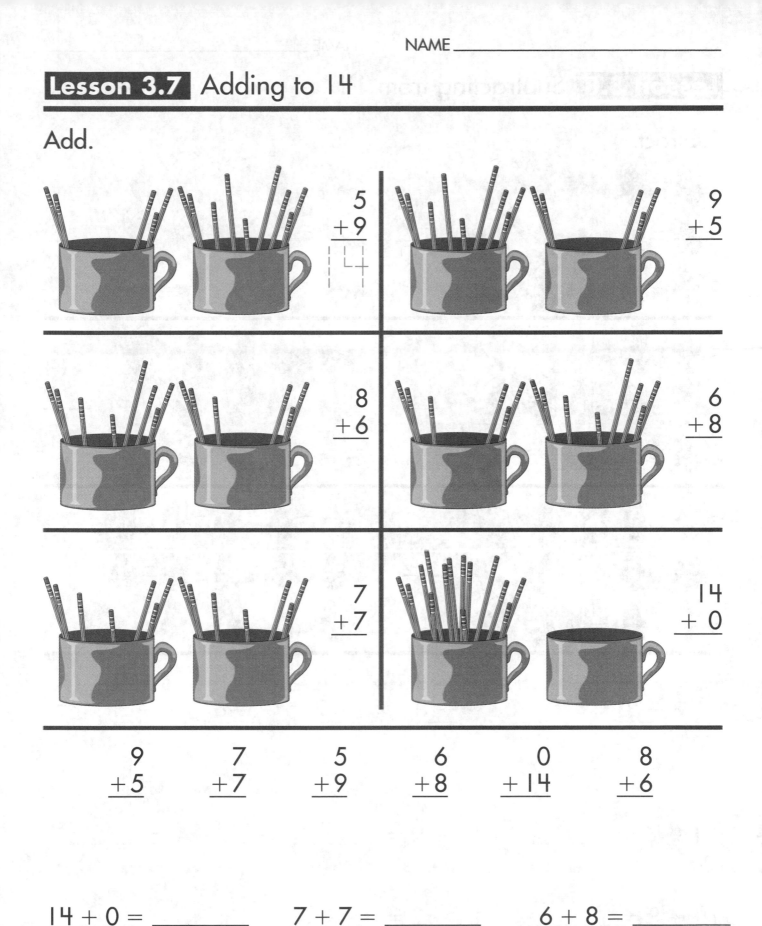

$\begin{array}{r} 5 \\ +9 \\ \hline 14 \end{array}$

$\begin{array}{r} 9 \\ +5 \\ \hline \end{array}$

$\begin{array}{r} 8 \\ +6 \\ \hline \end{array}$

$\begin{array}{r} 6 \\ +8 \\ \hline \end{array}$

$\begin{array}{r} 7 \\ +7 \\ \hline \end{array}$

$\begin{array}{r} 14 \\ +0 \\ \hline \end{array}$

$\begin{array}{r} 9 \\ +5 \\ \hline \end{array}$
$\begin{array}{r} 7 \\ +7 \\ \hline \end{array}$
$\begin{array}{r} 5 \\ +9 \\ \hline \end{array}$
$\begin{array}{r} 6 \\ +8 \\ \hline \end{array}$
$\begin{array}{r} 0 \\ +14 \\ \hline \end{array}$
$\begin{array}{r} 8 \\ +6 \\ \hline \end{array}$

$14 + 0 = $ _____ $7 + 7 = $ _____ $6 + 8 = $ _____

Lesson 3.8 Subtracting from 14

Subtract.

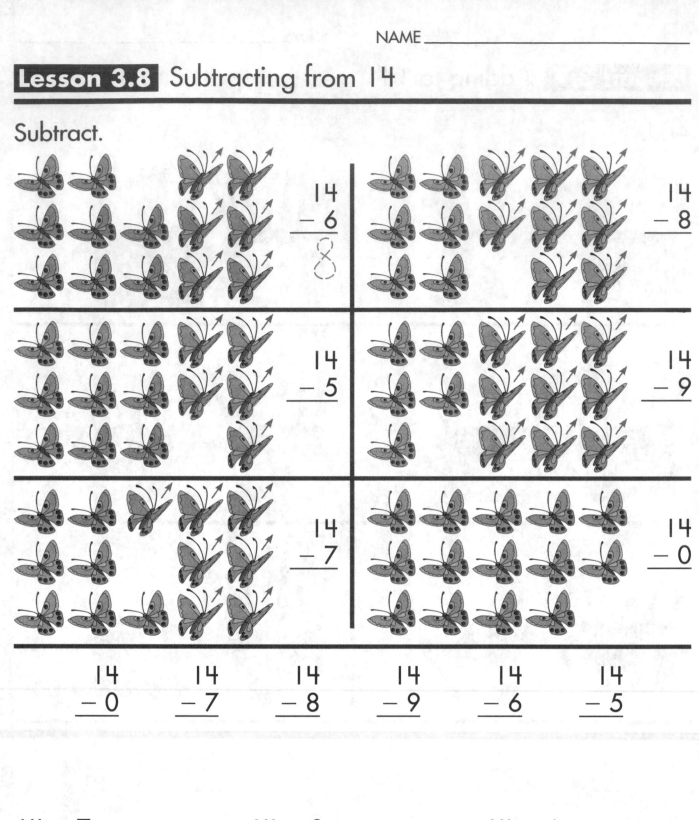

$$\begin{array}{r} 14 \\ -\ 6 \\ \hline 8 \end{array}$$

$$\begin{array}{r} 14 \\ -\ 8 \\ \hline \end{array}$$

$$\begin{array}{r} 14 \\ -\ 5 \\ \hline \end{array}$$

$$\begin{array}{r} 14 \\ -\ 9 \\ \hline \end{array}$$

$$\begin{array}{r} 14 \\ -\ 7 \\ \hline \end{array}$$

$$\begin{array}{r} 14 \\ -\ 0 \\ \hline \end{array}$$

$$\begin{array}{r} 14 \\ -\ 0 \\ \hline \end{array} \qquad \begin{array}{r} 14 \\ -\ 7 \\ \hline \end{array} \qquad \begin{array}{r} 14 \\ -\ 8 \\ \hline \end{array} \qquad \begin{array}{r} 14 \\ -\ 9 \\ \hline \end{array} \qquad \begin{array}{r} 14 \\ -\ 6 \\ \hline \end{array} \qquad \begin{array}{r} 14 \\ -\ 5 \\ \hline \end{array}$$

$14 - 7 =$ _____ $14 - 9 =$ _____ $14 - 6 =$ _____

$14 - 8 =$ _____ $14 - 2 =$ _____ $14 - 3 =$ _____

Lesson 3.9 Fact Families 11 through 15

Add or subtract.

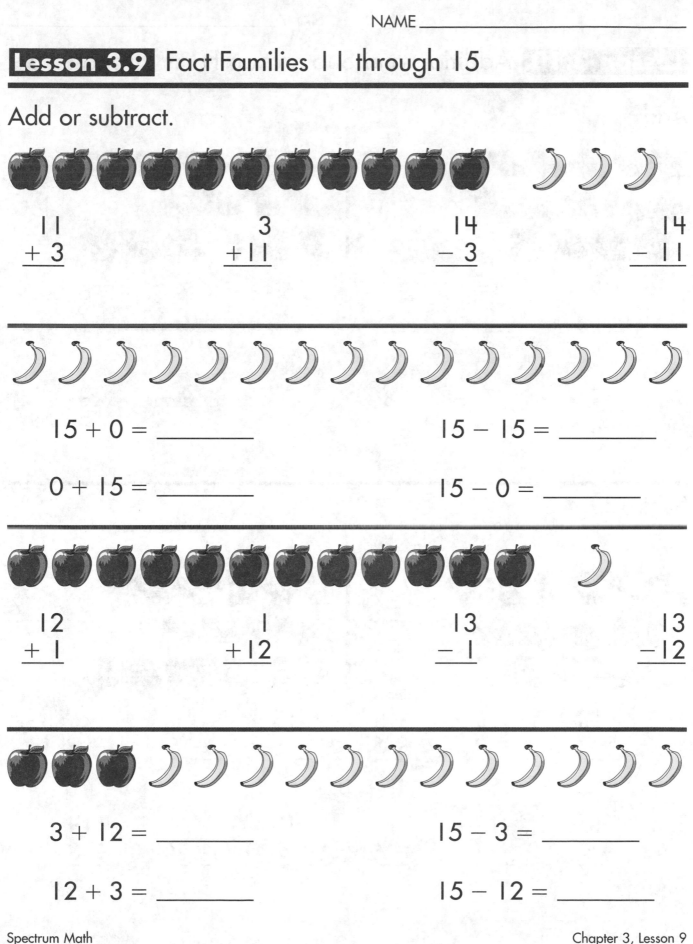

$$\begin{array}{r} 11 \\ + 3 \\ \hline \end{array}$$
$$\begin{array}{r} 3 \\ + 11 \\ \hline \end{array}$$
$$\begin{array}{r} 14 \\ - 3 \\ \hline \end{array}$$
$$\begin{array}{r} 14 \\ - 11 \\ \hline \end{array}$$

$15 + 0 = $ _____ $15 - 15 = $ _____

$0 + 15 = $ _____ $15 - 0 = $ _____

$$\begin{array}{r} 12 \\ + 1 \\ \hline \end{array}$$
$$\begin{array}{r} 1 \\ + 12 \\ \hline \end{array}$$
$$\begin{array}{r} 13 \\ - 1 \\ \hline \end{array}$$
$$\begin{array}{r} 13 \\ - 12 \\ \hline \end{array}$$

$3 + 12 = $ _____ $15 - 3 = $ _____

$12 + 3 = $ _____ $15 - 12 = $ _____

Lesson 3.10 Addition and Subtraction Facts through 15

Add.

$$\begin{array}{r} 6 \\ +9 \\ \hline 15 \end{array}$$

$$\begin{array}{r} 9 \\ +6 \\ \hline 15 \end{array}$$

$$\begin{array}{r} 7 \\ +8 \\ \hline \end{array}$$
$$\begin{array}{r} 9 \\ +5 \\ \hline \end{array}$$
$$\begin{array}{r} 6 \\ +9 \\ \hline \end{array}$$
$$\begin{array}{r} 5 \\ +8 \\ \hline \end{array}$$
$$\begin{array}{r} 7 \\ +7 \\ \hline \end{array}$$
$$\begin{array}{r} 6 \\ +7 \\ \hline \end{array}$$

$$\begin{array}{r} 9 \\ +6 \\ \hline \end{array}$$
$$\begin{array}{r} 7 \\ +6 \\ \hline \end{array}$$
$$\begin{array}{r} 8 \\ +7 \\ \hline \end{array}$$
$$\begin{array}{r} 7 \\ +7 \\ \hline \end{array}$$
$$\begin{array}{r} 8 \\ +6 \\ \hline \end{array}$$
$$\begin{array}{r} 4 \\ +9 \\ \hline \end{array}$$

Subtract.

$$\begin{array}{r} 15 \\ -9 \\ \hline 6 \end{array}$$

$$\begin{array}{r} 15 \\ -6 \\ \hline 9 \end{array}$$

$$\begin{array}{r} 13 \\ -7 \\ \hline \end{array}$$
$$\begin{array}{r} 15 \\ -8 \\ \hline \end{array}$$
$$\begin{array}{r} 14 \\ -5 \\ \hline \end{array}$$
$$\begin{array}{r} 13 \\ -8 \\ \hline \end{array}$$
$$\begin{array}{r} 14 \\ -6 \\ \hline \end{array}$$
$$\begin{array}{r} 15 \\ -9 \\ \hline \end{array}$$

$$\begin{array}{r} 15 \\ -7 \\ \hline \end{array}$$
$$\begin{array}{r} 13 \\ -4 \\ \hline \end{array}$$
$$\begin{array}{r} 15 \\ -6 \\ \hline \end{array}$$
$$\begin{array}{r} 13 \\ -9 \\ \hline \end{array}$$
$$\begin{array}{r} 14 \\ -7 \\ \hline \end{array}$$
$$\begin{array}{r} 14 \\ -8 \\ \hline \end{array}$$

Lesson 3.10 Problem Solving

Solve each problem.

There are 15 🚗.

9 🚓 drive away.

How many 🚙 are left? _____6_____

$$\begin{array}{r} 15 \\ -\ 9 \\ \hline 6 \end{array}$$

There are 7 🍁.

There are 8 🍂.

How many leaves in all? _____

There are 9 🧸 on the shelf.

There are 6 more 🧸 on the floor.

How many 🧸 in all? _____

Marcus has 15 ⚾.

Sue has 7 ⚾.

How many more ⚾ does Marcus have? _____

Len has 15 ✈.

He has 6 🚚.

How many more ✈ does he have? _____

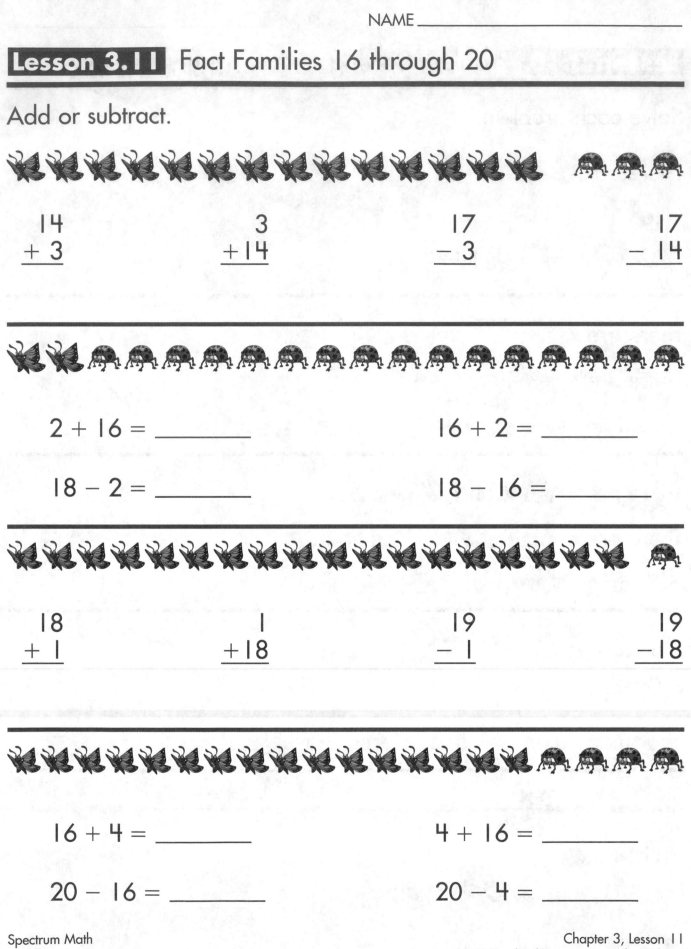

Add or subtract.

$$\begin{array}{r} 14 \\ + 3 \\ \hline \end{array} \qquad \begin{array}{r} 3 \\ +14 \\ \hline \end{array} \qquad \begin{array}{r} 17 \\ - 3 \\ \hline \end{array} \qquad \begin{array}{r} 17 \\ -14 \\ \hline \end{array}$$

$2 + 16 =$ _____ $16 + 2 =$ _____

$18 - 2 =$ _____ $18 - 16 =$ _____

$$\begin{array}{r} 18 \\ + 1 \\ \hline \end{array} \qquad \begin{array}{r} 1 \\ +18 \\ \hline \end{array} \qquad \begin{array}{r} 19 \\ - 1 \\ \hline \end{array} \qquad \begin{array}{r} 19 \\ -18 \\ \hline \end{array}$$

$16 + 4 =$ _____ $4 + 16 =$ _____

$20 - 16 =$ _____ $20 - 4 =$ _____

Lesson 3.12 Addition and Subtraction Facts through 16

Add.

$$\begin{array}{r} 7 \\ +9 \\ \hline 16 \end{array}$$

$$\begin{array}{r} 9 \\ +7 \\ \hline 16 \end{array}$$

$$\begin{array}{r} 7 \\ +7 \\ \hline \end{array} \quad \begin{array}{r} 8 \\ +8 \\ \hline \end{array} \quad \begin{array}{r} 7 \\ +8 \\ \hline \end{array} \quad \begin{array}{r} 9 \\ +7 \\ \hline \end{array} \quad \begin{array}{r} 5 \\ +9 \\ \hline \end{array} \quad \begin{array}{r} 9 \\ +6 \\ \hline \end{array}$$

$$\begin{array}{r} 6 \\ +9 \\ \hline \end{array} \quad \begin{array}{r} 6 \\ +8 \\ \hline \end{array} \quad \begin{array}{r} 7 \\ +9 \\ \hline \end{array} \quad \begin{array}{r} 9 \\ +5 \\ \hline \end{array} \quad \begin{array}{r} 8 \\ +6 \\ \hline \end{array} \quad \begin{array}{r} 8 \\ +7 \\ \hline \end{array}$$

Subtract.

$$\begin{array}{r} 16 \\ -9 \\ \hline 7 \end{array}$$

$$\begin{array}{r} 16 \\ -7 \\ \hline 9 \end{array}$$

$$\begin{array}{r} 15 \\ -7 \\ \hline \end{array} \quad \begin{array}{r} 16 \\ -8 \\ \hline \end{array} \quad \begin{array}{r} 14 \\ -9 \\ \hline \end{array} \quad \begin{array}{r} 15 \\ -9 \\ \hline \end{array} \quad \begin{array}{r} 14 \\ -7 \\ \hline \end{array} \quad \begin{array}{r} 16 \\ -7 \\ \hline \end{array}$$

$$\begin{array}{r} 15 \\ -6 \\ \hline \end{array} \quad \begin{array}{r} 14 \\ -8 \\ \hline \end{array} \quad \begin{array}{r} 16 \\ -9 \\ \hline \end{array} \quad \begin{array}{r} 14 \\ -5 \\ \hline \end{array} \quad \begin{array}{r} 15 \\ -8 \\ \hline \end{array} \quad \begin{array}{r} 14 \\ -6 \\ \hline \end{array}$$

Lesson 3.12 Problem Solving

SHOW YOUR WORK

Solve each problem.

There are 9 🐱.

There are 7 🐿️.

How many in all? ___16___

$$\begin{array}{r} 9 \\ + 7 \\ \hline 16 \end{array}$$

There are 16 🥜.

Ted eats 8 🥜.

How many 🥜 are left? _____

Ivan has 16 📕.

He has read 7 📕.

How many 📕 does Ivan still need to read? _____

Aisha has 8 🧸.

She has 8 🧸.

How many in all? _____

There are 7 🦛.

9 more 🦛 come.

How many 🦛 are there? _____

Lesson 3.13 Using Addition for Subtraction

Think addition for subtraction. Solve each problem.

17 🚂 − 3 🚂 = _____ | 3 🚂 + _____ = 17 🚂

20 🍑 − 5 🍑 = _____ | 5 🍑 + _____ = 20 🍑

19 🐿 − 5 🐿 = _____ | 5 🐿 + _____ = 19 🐿

18 🐸 − 1 🐸 = _____ | 1 🐸 + _____ = 18 🐸

15 🐟 − 4 🐟 = _____ | 4 🐟 + _____ = 15 🐟

14 🦒 − 2 🦒 = _____ | 2 🦒 + _____ = 14 🦒

16 🐄 − 1 🐄 = _____ | 1 🐄 + _____ = 16 🐄

20 🐐 − 6 🐐 = _____ | 6 🐐 + _____ = 20 🐐

13 🦛 − 0 🦛 = _____ | 0 🦛 + _____ = 13 🦛

Lesson 3.14 Addition and Subtraction Facts through 18

Add.

$$\begin{array}{r} 8 \\ +9 \\ \hline 17 \end{array} \qquad \begin{array}{r} 9 \\ +9 \\ \hline 18 \end{array}$$

$$\begin{array}{r} 8 \\ +8 \\ \hline \end{array} \qquad \begin{array}{r} 9 \\ +8 \\ \hline \end{array} \qquad \begin{array}{r} 5 \\ +9 \\ \hline \end{array} \qquad \begin{array}{r} 7 \\ +8 \\ \hline \end{array} \qquad \begin{array}{r} 9 \\ +9 \\ \hline \end{array} \qquad \begin{array}{r} 8 \\ +6 \\ \hline \end{array}$$

$$\begin{array}{r} 6 \\ +9 \\ \hline \end{array} \qquad \begin{array}{r} 7 \\ +7 \\ \hline \end{array} \qquad \begin{array}{r} 8 \\ +9 \\ \hline \end{array} \qquad \begin{array}{r} 8 \\ +7 \\ \hline \end{array} \qquad \begin{array}{r} 9 \\ +7 \\ \hline \end{array} \qquad \begin{array}{r} 9 \\ +6 \\ \hline \end{array}$$

Subtract.

$$\begin{array}{r} 17 \\ -9 \\ \hline 8 \end{array} \qquad \begin{array}{r} 17 \\ -8 \\ \hline 9 \end{array} \qquad \begin{array}{r} 18 \\ -9 \\ \hline 9 \end{array}$$

$$\begin{array}{r} 15 \\ -8 \\ \hline \end{array} \qquad \begin{array}{r} 17 \\ -9 \\ \hline \end{array} \qquad \begin{array}{r} 14 \\ -7 \\ \hline \end{array} \qquad \begin{array}{r} 18 \\ -9 \\ \hline \end{array} \qquad \begin{array}{r} 16 \\ -7 \\ \hline \end{array} \qquad \begin{array}{r} 15 \\ -6 \\ \hline \end{array}$$

$$\begin{array}{r} 17 \\ -8 \\ \hline \end{array} \qquad \begin{array}{r} 14 \\ -6 \\ \hline \end{array} \qquad \begin{array}{r} 16 \\ -9 \\ \hline \end{array} \qquad \begin{array}{r} 16 \\ -8 \\ \hline \end{array} \qquad \begin{array}{r} 15 \\ -7 \\ \hline \end{array} \qquad \begin{array}{r} 14 \\ -5 \\ \hline \end{array}$$

Lesson 3.14 Problem Solving

SHOW YOUR WORK

Solve each problem.

There are 17 ✏.

9 ✏ are broken.

How many ✏ are not broken? ___8___

$$\begin{array}{r} 17 \\ -9 \\ \hline 8 \end{array}$$

There are 9 🐞.

9 more 🐞 come.

How many 🐞 are there? _____

Luisa caught 8 🐟.

She catches 9 more 🐟.

How many 🐟 did she catch in all? _____

There are 18 🐰.

9 🐰 run away.

How many 🐰 are left? _____

There are 17 🔨.

There are 8 🍴.

How many more 🔨 are there? _____

Lesson 3.15 Using Addition for Subtraction

Think addition for subtraction. Solve each problem.

20 🐌 − 7 🐌 = _____   7 🐌 + _____ = 20 🐌

18 🏈 − 5 🏈 = _____   5 🏈 + _____ = 18 🏈

19 ⚾ − 7 ⚾ = _____   7 ⚾ + _____ = 19 ⚾

17 🌼 − 6 🌼 = _____   6 🌼 + _____ = 17 🌼

16 🚗 − 4 🚗 = _____   4 🚗 + _____ = 16 🚗

12 🚚 − 1 🚚 = _____   1 🚚 + _____ = 12 🚚

15 ✈ − 3 ✈ = _____   3 ✈ + _____ = 15 ✈

14 🐕 − 3 🐕 = _____   3 🐕 + _____ = 14 🐕

20 🐁 − 8 🐁 = _____   8 🐁 + _____ = 20 🐁

Lesson 3.16 More- and Less-Than Facts 11 through 20

Add to find more than. Subtract to find less than.

How many is 2 more than 10 🍑? _____

What is 3 more than 16 🐐? _____

There are 5 less than 15 🐸. How many 🐸 are there? _____

What is 4 less than 14 🐌? _____

There are 4 more than 13 🐕. How many 🐕 are there? _____

What is 2 less than 17 ⚾? _____

How many is 1 less than 19 🦛? _____

How many is 5 more than 12 🌼? _____

There are 4 less than 20 🐰. How many 🐰 are there? _____

Check What You Learned

Addition and Subtraction Facts through 20

Add.

8 +7	8 +9	6 +7	14 +5	3 +8	9 +5
9 +3	5 +8	7 +9	11 +9	8 +4	9 +9
7 +5	7 +8	4 +9	2 +9	6 +9	8 +6

Subtract.

14 − 5	15 − 7	19 − 6	12 − 4	16 − 9	11 − 3
17 − 8	14 − 7	12 − 6	13 − 5	11 − 7	18 − 9
13 − 9	15 − 8	16 − 7	17 − 9	12 − 8	20 − 9

Check What You Learned

Addition and Subtraction Facts through 20

Solve each problem.

There are 20 🧢.

There are 8 👒.

What is the difference? _____

There are 7 🥄 on the table.

There are 6 🥄 in the drawer.

How many 🥄 in all? _____

There are 18 🍎.

We eat 9 🍎.

How many 🍎 are left? _____

There are 6 🦁.

9 more 🦁 come.

How many 🦁 are there in all? _____

Tanya has 9 🌼.

Curtis has 7 🌼.

How many 🌼 do they have in all? _____

NAME _____

Check What You Know

Addition and Subtraction Facts through 100

Add.

17	18	12	20	19
+ 4	+ 2	+ 3	+ 1	+ 6

14	39	42	21	18
+10	+20	+30	+10	+30

Subtract.

60	30	90	70	20
−30	−30	−20	−40	−10

80	90	50	40	80
−50	−70	−20	−10	−60

Add.

12	10	14	8	4
3	5	2	9	7
+2	+5	+3	+1	+6

3	5	4	10	11
2	1	4	1	2
+1	+3	+2	+4	+2

Lesson 4.1 Adding 2-Digit and 1-Digit Numbers

First add ones.   Then, add tens.

$$25 \atop + \; 3$$

$$25 \atop \underline{+ \; 3} \atop 8$$

$$25 \atop \underline{+ \; 3}$$
sum = 28

Add the ones.	Put the ones in the ones place. Put the ten in the tens place.	Add the tens.
$38 \atop \underline{+4} \atop ?$ $8 \atop \underline{+4} \atop 12$ 12 = 1 ten and 2 ones	$\overset{1}{38} \atop \underline{+4} \atop 2$	$\overset{1}{38} \atop \underline{+4}$ sum = 42

Add.

$15 \atop \underline{+2}$	$19 \atop \underline{+6}$	$27 \atop \underline{+5}$	$20 \atop \underline{+6}$	$13 \atop \underline{+4}$
$38 \atop \underline{+8}$	$22 \atop \underline{+6}$	$29 \atop \underline{+3}$	$47 \atop \underline{+2}$	$14 \atop \underline{+1}$
$63 \atop \underline{+5}$	$53 \atop \underline{+6}$	$87 \atop \underline{+2}$	$41 \atop \underline{+4}$	$79 \atop \underline{+9}$

Lesson 4.1 Adding 2-Digit and 1-Digit Numbers

Add.

63 + 6 69	42 + 5 47	29 + 9	71 + 8	62 + 3
45 + 4	19 + 6	30 + 9	16 + 7	22 + 4
30 + 6	81 + 7	47 + 2	56 + 5	48 + 7
15 + 8	67 + 1	42 + 3	56 + 4	39 + 5
23 + 8	17 + 7	44 + 6	16 + 3	86 + 6
90 + 4	31 + 9	68 + 4	24 + 5	36 + 8

Lesson 4.2 Adding Multiples of 10 to 2-Digit Numbers

6 tens and 8 ones plus 2 tens equals 8 tens and 8 ones.

$$\begin{array}{r} 68 \\ +20 \\ \hline 88 \end{array}$$

↑

Only the tens
place changes.

Add.

$$\begin{array}{r} 15 \\ +10 \\ \hline \end{array}$$
$$\begin{array}{r} 19 \\ +20 \\ \hline \end{array}$$
$$\begin{array}{r} 23 \\ +20 \\ \hline \end{array}$$
$$\begin{array}{r} 31 \\ +10 \\ \hline \end{array}$$
$$\begin{array}{r} 47 \\ +20 \\ \hline \end{array}$$

$$\begin{array}{r} 13 \\ +30 \\ \hline \end{array}$$
$$\begin{array}{r} 29 \\ +40 \\ \hline \end{array}$$
$$\begin{array}{r} 17 \\ +40 \\ \hline \end{array}$$
$$\begin{array}{r} 11 \\ +50 \\ \hline \end{array}$$
$$\begin{array}{r} 60 \\ +30 \\ \hline \end{array}$$

$$\begin{array}{r} 75 \\ +10 \\ \hline \end{array}$$
$$\begin{array}{r} 50 \\ +40 \\ \hline \end{array}$$
$$\begin{array}{r} 25 \\ +70 \\ \hline \end{array}$$
$$\begin{array}{r} 42 \\ +50 \\ \hline \end{array}$$
$$\begin{array}{r} 12 \\ +80 \\ \hline \end{array}$$

$$\begin{array}{r} 18 \\ +20 \\ \hline \end{array}$$
$$\begin{array}{r} 12 \\ +80 \\ \hline \end{array}$$
$$\begin{array}{r} 20 \\ +40 \\ \hline \end{array}$$
$$\begin{array}{r} 59 \\ +20 \\ \hline \end{array}$$
$$\begin{array}{r} 15 \\ +70 \\ \hline \end{array}$$

$$\begin{array}{r} 17 \\ +40 \\ \hline \end{array}$$
$$\begin{array}{r} 11 \\ +20 \\ \hline \end{array}$$
$$\begin{array}{r} 49 \\ +30 \\ \hline \end{array}$$
$$\begin{array}{r} 86 \\ +10 \\ \hline \end{array}$$
$$\begin{array}{r} 25 \\ +70 \\ \hline \end{array}$$

Lesson 4.3 Problem Solving

Solve each problem.

There are 23 🐛 .

10 more 🐛 are blown up.

How many 🐛 are there now? __33__

$$\begin{array}{r} 23 \\ + 10 \\ \hline 33 \end{array}$$

There are 15 🍑 in a basket.

There are 9 🍑 in a bowl.

How many 🍑 in all? _____

There are 31 🦢 in the pond.

7 🦢 are on the grass.

How many 🦢 in all? _____

There are 27 ✏ on the table.

There are 6 ✏ in the box.

How many ✏ in all? _____

There are 56 🍁 on the ground.

20 more 🍁 fall.

How many 🍁 are on the ground now? _____

There are 34 🐕 in the dog park.

30 more 🐕 come.

What is 34 plus 30? _____

Lesson 4.4 Subtracting Multiples of 10

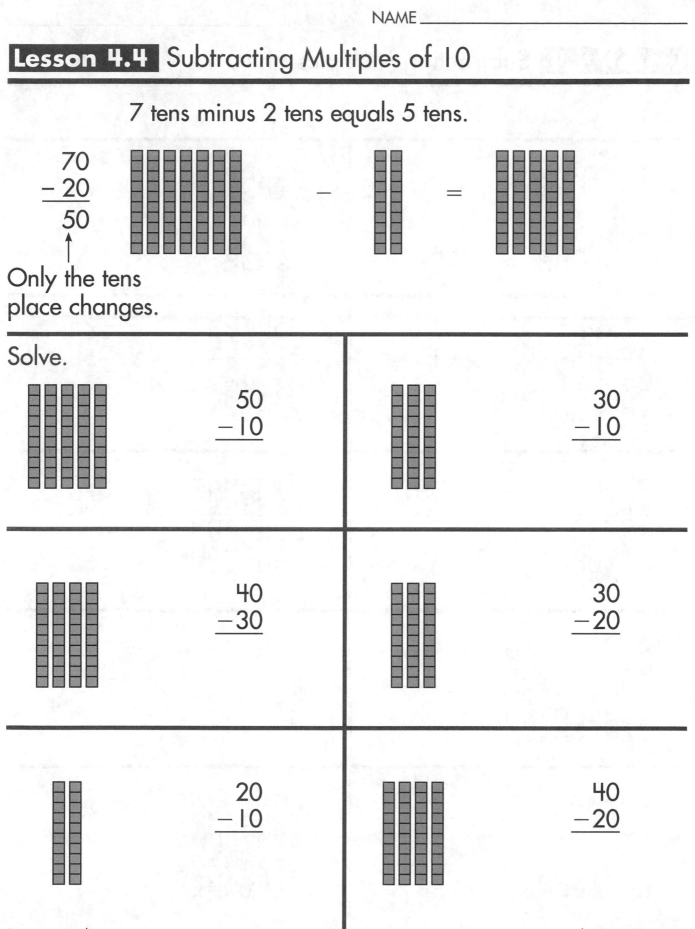

7 tens minus 2 tens equals 5 tens.

$$\begin{array}{r} 70 \\ -\ 20 \\ \hline 50 \end{array}$$

↑

Only the tens
place changes.

Solve.

$$\begin{array}{r} 50 \\ -10 \\ \hline \end{array}$$

$$\begin{array}{r} 30 \\ -10 \\ \hline \end{array}$$

$$\begin{array}{r} 40 \\ -30 \\ \hline \end{array}$$

$$\begin{array}{r} 30 \\ -20 \\ \hline \end{array}$$

$$\begin{array}{r} 20 \\ -10 \\ \hline \end{array}$$

$$\begin{array}{r} 40 \\ -20 \\ \hline \end{array}$$

Lesson 4.4 Subtracting Multiples of 10

Solve.

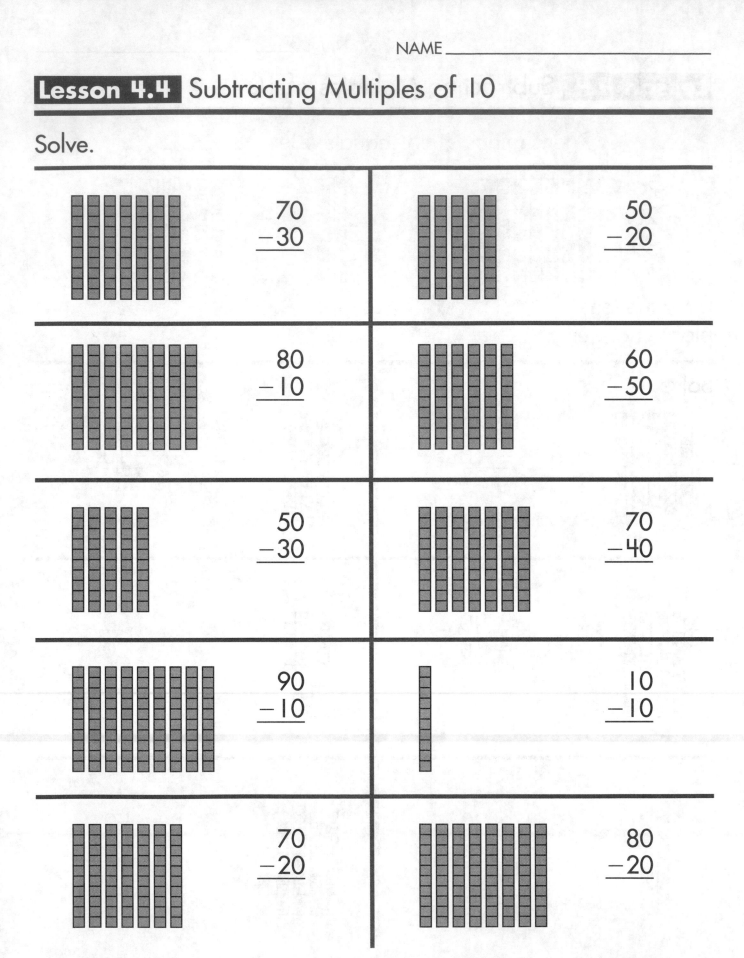

$\begin{array}{r} 70 \\ -30 \\ \hline \end{array}$	$\begin{array}{r} 50 \\ -20 \\ \hline \end{array}$
$\begin{array}{r} 80 \\ -10 \\ \hline \end{array}$	$\begin{array}{r} 60 \\ -50 \\ \hline \end{array}$
$\begin{array}{r} 50 \\ -30 \\ \hline \end{array}$	$\begin{array}{r} 70 \\ -40 \\ \hline \end{array}$
$\begin{array}{r} 90 \\ -10 \\ \hline \end{array}$	$\begin{array}{r} 10 \\ -10 \\ \hline \end{array}$
$\begin{array}{r} 70 \\ -20 \\ \hline \end{array}$	$\begin{array}{r} 80 \\ -20 \\ \hline \end{array}$

Lesson 4.5 Addition and Subtraction Practice through 100

Add.

9 +8	9 +7	16 +9	27 +8	28 +5	37 +7
17					

49 +9	67 +9	58 +7	18 +9	78 +6	96 +4

87 +6	29 +5	79 +6	8 +8	46 +8	66 +7

Subtract.

20 −10	70 −60	40 −20	80 −70	60 −10	80 −60

90 −80	50 −10	20 −20	40 −10	90 −40	90 −60

60 −60	30 −20	70 −10	40 −20	60 −50	80 −20

Lesson 4.5 Problem Solving

SHOW YOUR WORK

Solve each problem.

There are 30 🐦.

Ten 🐦 fly away.

How many are left? ___20___

$$\begin{array}{r} 30 \\ -10 \\ \hline 20 \end{array}$$

I have 19 🍌.

I have 6 🔴.

What is the sum? _____

There are 40 🧃.

We drink 10 🧃.

How many are left? _____

There are 38 🚗.

8 more 🚗 drive up.

How many 🚗 are there in all? _____

I want 80 ✏.

I have 30 ✏.

How many more do I need? _____

Lesson 4.6 Adding Three Numbers

	Add the ones.	Add the tens.
12 ▯▯▯▯▯▯▯▯▯▯ ▯▯	↓	↓
4 ▯▯▯▯	12	12
+3 ▯▯▯	4	4
9	+3	+3
	9	sum = 19

Add.

$$
\begin{array}{r} 10 \\ 5 \\ + 3 \\ \hline \end{array}
\qquad
\begin{array}{r} 11 \\ 3 \\ + 5 \\ \hline \end{array}
\qquad
\begin{array}{r} 4 \\ 3 \\ + 2 \\ \hline \end{array}
\qquad
\begin{array}{r} 15 \\ 3 \\ + 2 \\ \hline \end{array}
\qquad
\begin{array}{r} 2 \\ 2 \\ + 2 \\ \hline \end{array}
$$

$$
\begin{array}{r} 2 \\ 4 \\ + 1 \\ \hline \end{array}
\qquad
\begin{array}{r} 8 \\ 2 \\ + 1 \\ \hline \end{array}
\qquad
\begin{array}{r} 12 \\ 4 \\ + 1 \\ \hline \end{array}
\qquad
\begin{array}{r} 2 \\ 3 \\ + 3 \\ \hline \end{array}
\qquad
\begin{array}{r} 1 \\ 1 \\ + 4 \\ \hline \end{array}
$$

$$
\begin{array}{r} 5 \\ 4 \\ + 1 \\ \hline \end{array}
\qquad
\begin{array}{r} 15 \\ 1 \\ + 1 \\ \hline \end{array}
\qquad
\begin{array}{r} 13 \\ 2 \\ + 1 \\ \hline \end{array}
\qquad
\begin{array}{r} 11 \\ 6 \\ + 2 \\ \hline \end{array}
\qquad
\begin{array}{r} 12 \\ 2 \\ + 6 \\ \hline \end{array}
$$

Lesson 4.6 Problem Solving

Solve each problem.

Lanie has 10 🦕.

Tina has 2 🦕. Paul has 5 🦕.

How many 🦕 do they have in all? _17_

$$\begin{array}{r} 10 \\ 2 \\ +5 \\ \hline 17 \end{array}$$

The toy store sold 7 🤖 in March,

3 🤖 in April, and 8 🤖 in May.

How many 🤖 did the toy store sell in all? _____

Felicia puts 2 🪆, 2 🧸, and

8 🐒 on shelves. How many toys

does Felicia put on shelves? _____

The toy store has 8 🚗, 2 🚚,

and 10 🪖. How many of these toys

does the toy store have in all? _____

The bakery sells 4 🧁 on Monday, 10 🧁

on Tuesday, and 6 🧁 on Wednesday.

How many 🧁 did the bakery sell? _____

Check What You Learned

Addition and Subtraction Facts through 100

Add.

12 + 4	18 + 2	15 + 3	17 + 1	13 + 6

25 +10	27 +20	33 +30	20 +10	48 +30

Subtract.

70 −30	30 −30	30 −20	50 −40	80 −10

70 −50	80 −70	70 −20	60 −10	60 −60

Add.

11 4 + 1	9 6 + 5	13 1 + 2	7 8 + 2	3 6 + 5

2 1 + 1	4 1 + 2	3 3 + 1	9 2 + 3	10 3 + 3

NAME _____

Check What You Know

Measurement

Write the time for each clock.

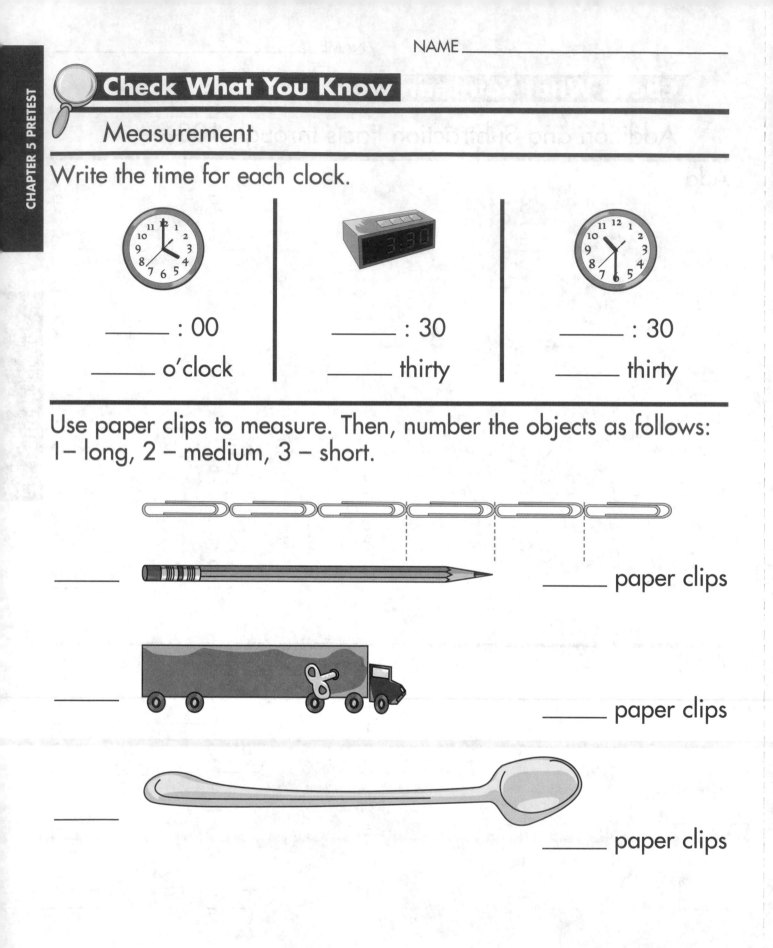

_____ : 00

_____ o'clock

_____ : 30

_____ thirty

_____ : 30

_____ thirty

Use paper clips to measure. Then, number the objects as follows:
1– long, 2 – medium, 3 – short.

_____   _____ paper clips

_____   _____ paper clips

_____   _____ paper clips

Check What You Know

Measurement

Use dimes to measure each object. Then, number the objects as follows: 1 – long, 2 – medium, 3 – short.

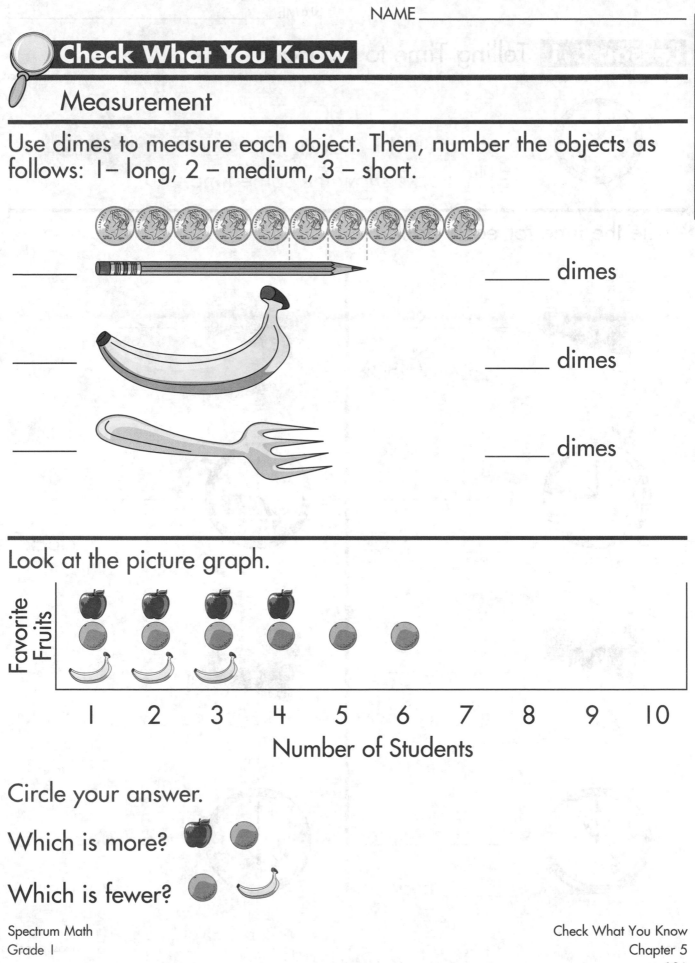

_____   _____ dimes

_____   _____ dimes

_____   _____ dimes

Look at the picture graph.

Circle your answer.

Which is more?

Which is fewer?

Lesson 5.1 Telling Time to the Hour

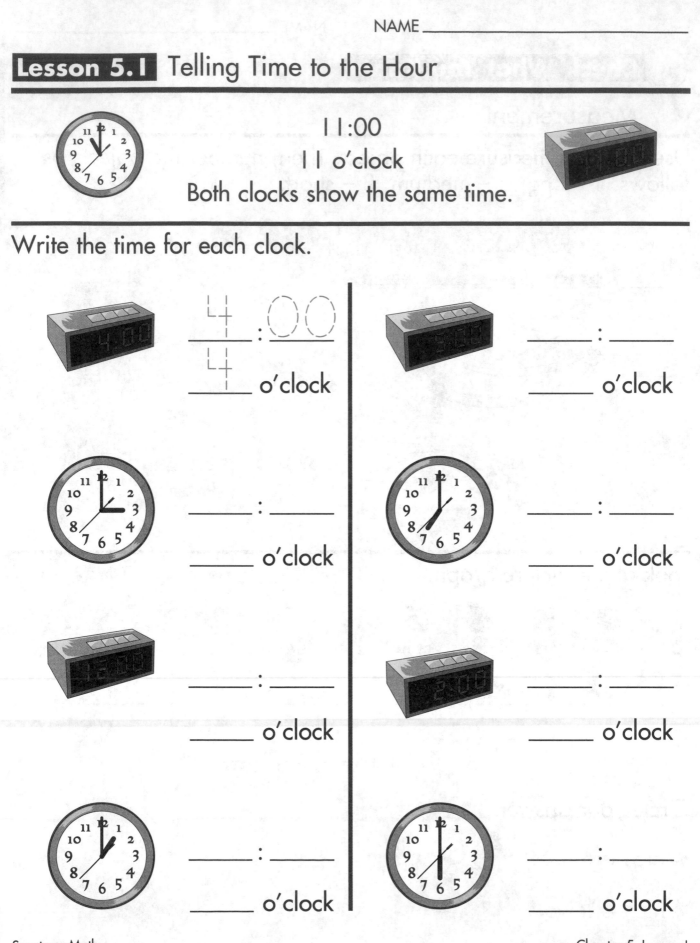

11:00
11 o'clock
Both clocks show the same time.

Write the time for each clock.

4:00
4 o'clock

___ : ___
___ o'clock

___ : ___
___ o'clock

___ : ___
___ o'clock

___ : ___
___ o'clock

___ : ___
___ o'clock

___ : ___
___ o'clock

___ : ___
___ o'clock

Lesson 5.1 Telling Time to the Hour

What time is it on the first clock?

Write this time on the second clock.

What time is it on the first clock?

Draw the hands to show this time on the second clock.

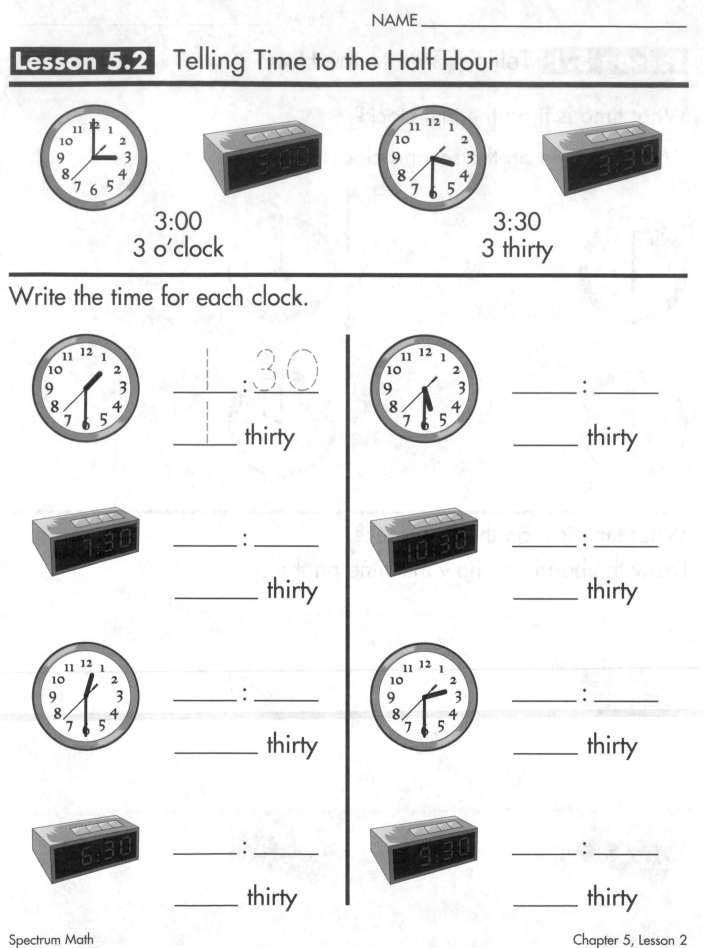

Lesson 5.2   Telling Time to the Half Hour

3:00
3 o'clock

3:30
3 thirty

Write the time for each clock.

_____:_30
_____ thirty

_____:_____
_____ thirty

7:30
_____:_____
_____ thirty

10:30
_____:_____
_____ thirty

_____:_____
_____ thirty

_____:_____
_____ thirty

6:30
_____:_____
_____ thirty

9:30
_____:_____
_____ thirty

Lesson 5.2 Telling Time to the Half Hour

What time is it on the first clock?

Write this time on the second clock.

What time is it on the first clock?

Draw the hands to show this time on the second clock.

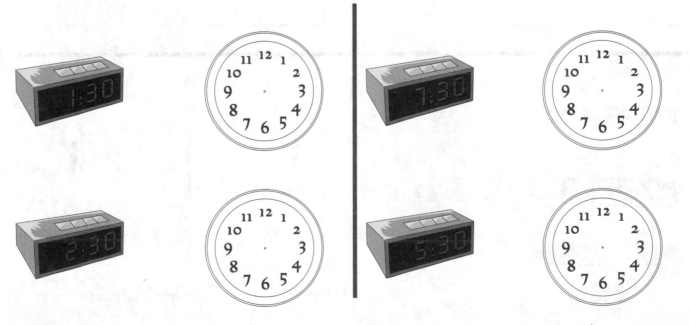

Lesson 5.3 Ordering Objects

Number the objects as follows: 1– long, 2 – medium, 3 – short

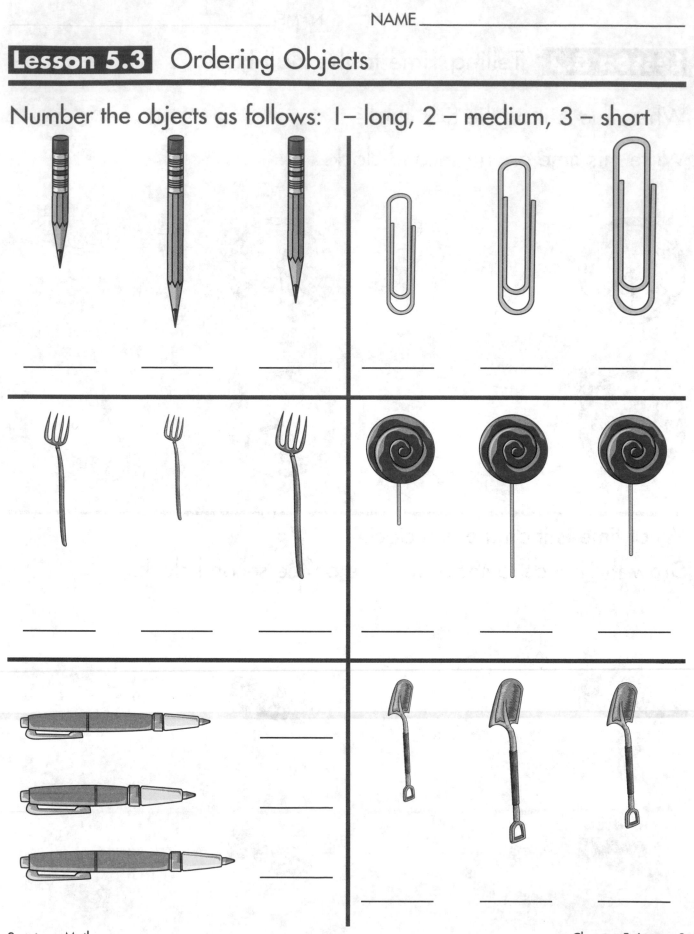

Lesson 5.3 Ordering Objects

Number the objects as follows: 1– long, 2 – medium, 3 – short

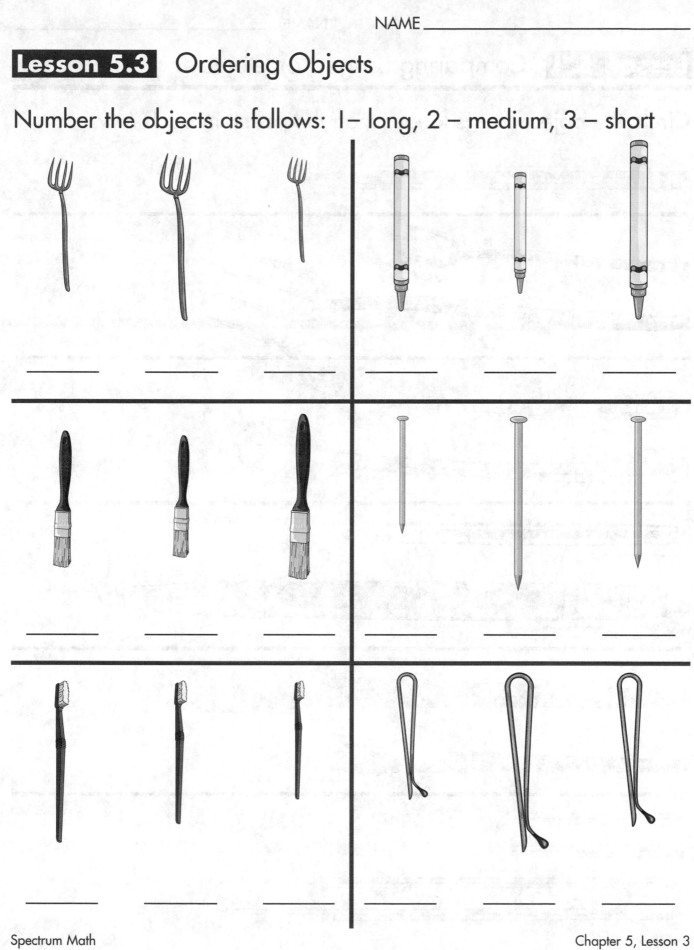

_____ _____ _____   _____ _____ _____

_____ _____ _____   _____ _____ _____

_____ _____ _____   _____ _____ _____

Lesson 5.4 Comparing Lengths of Objects

Circle the object that is longer than the pencil in each row.

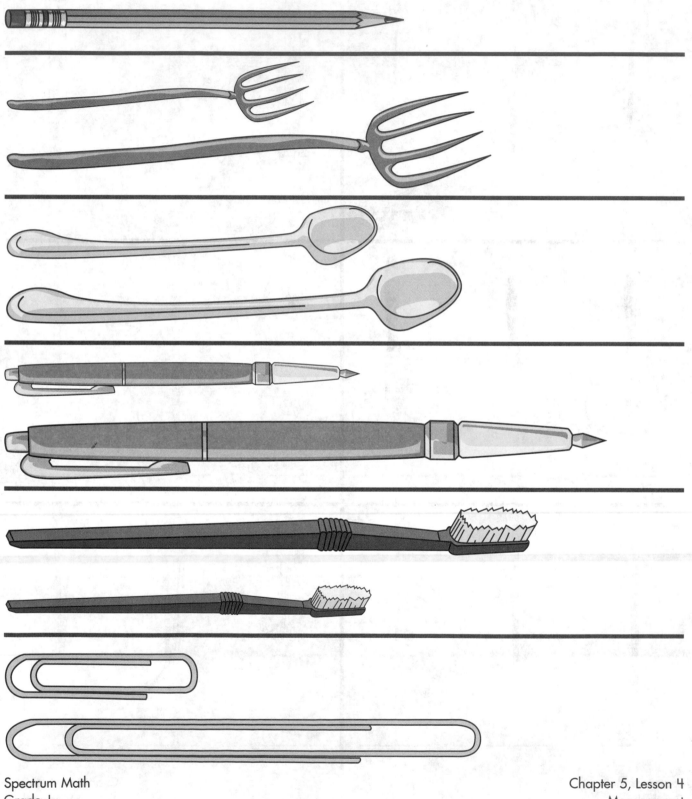

Lesson 5.4 Comparing Lengths of Objects

Circle the object that is shorter than the pencil in each row.

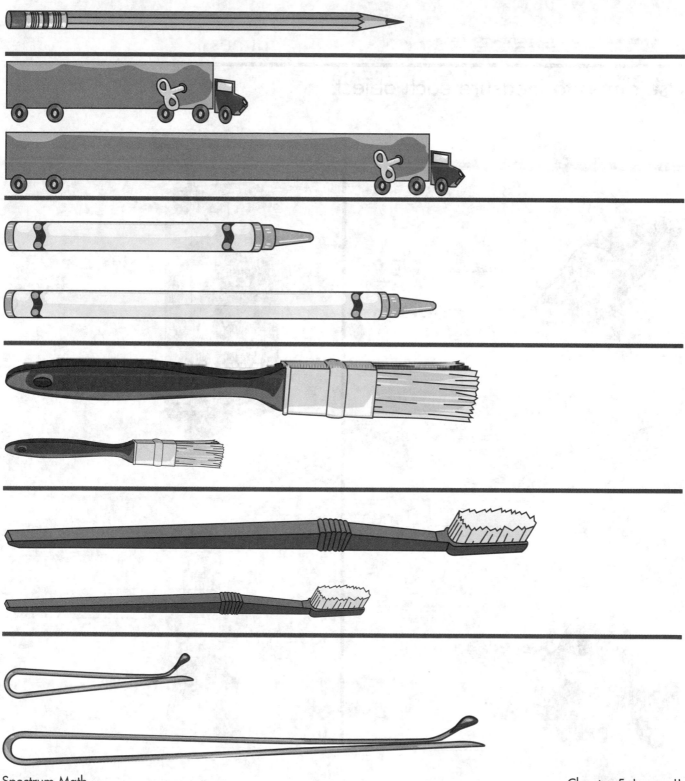

Lesson 5.5 Measuring Length and Height

Use dimes to measure.

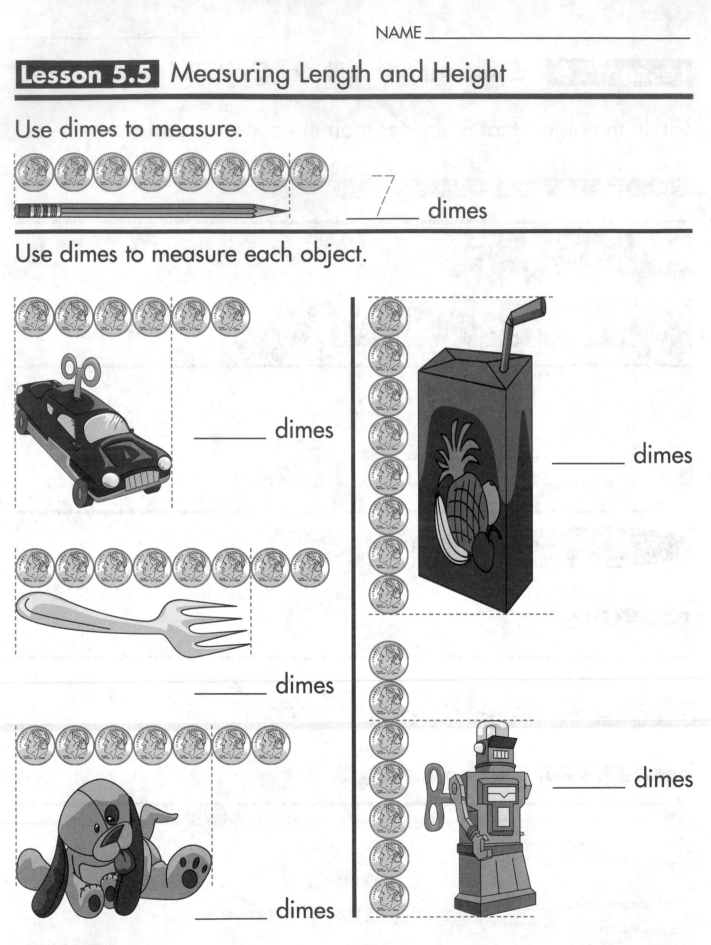

_____7_____ dimes

Use dimes to measure each object.

_____ dimes

_____ dimes

_____ dimes

_____ dimes

_____ dimes

_____ dimes

Lesson 5.5 Measuring Length and Height

Use paper clips to measure.

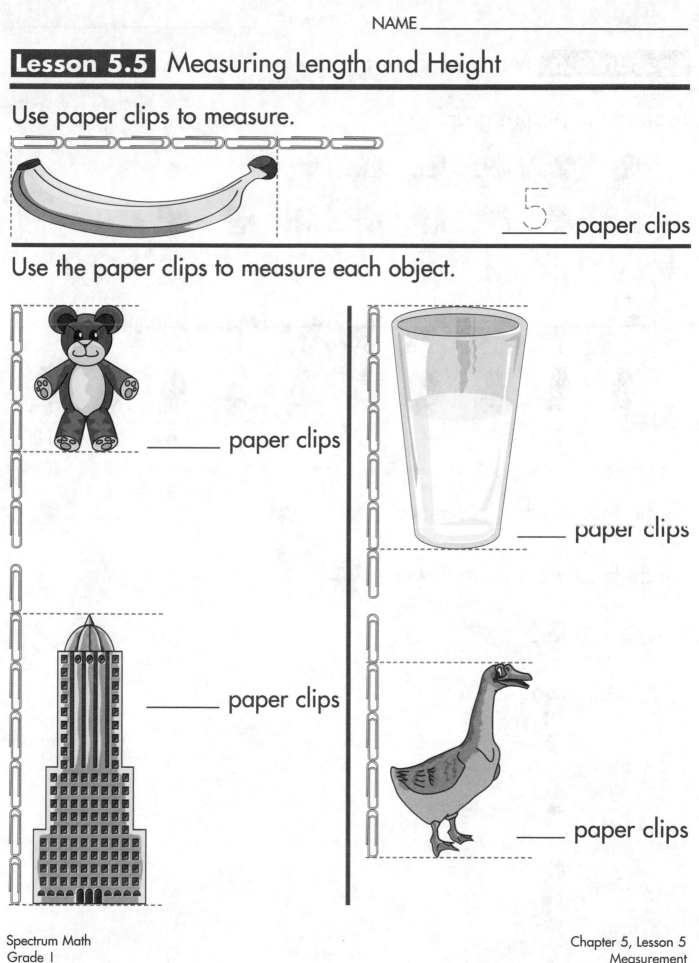

___5___ paper clips

Use the paper clips to measure each object.

_____ paper clips

_____ paper clips

_____ paper clips

_____ paper clips

Lesson 5.6 More or Fewer

Look at the picture graph.

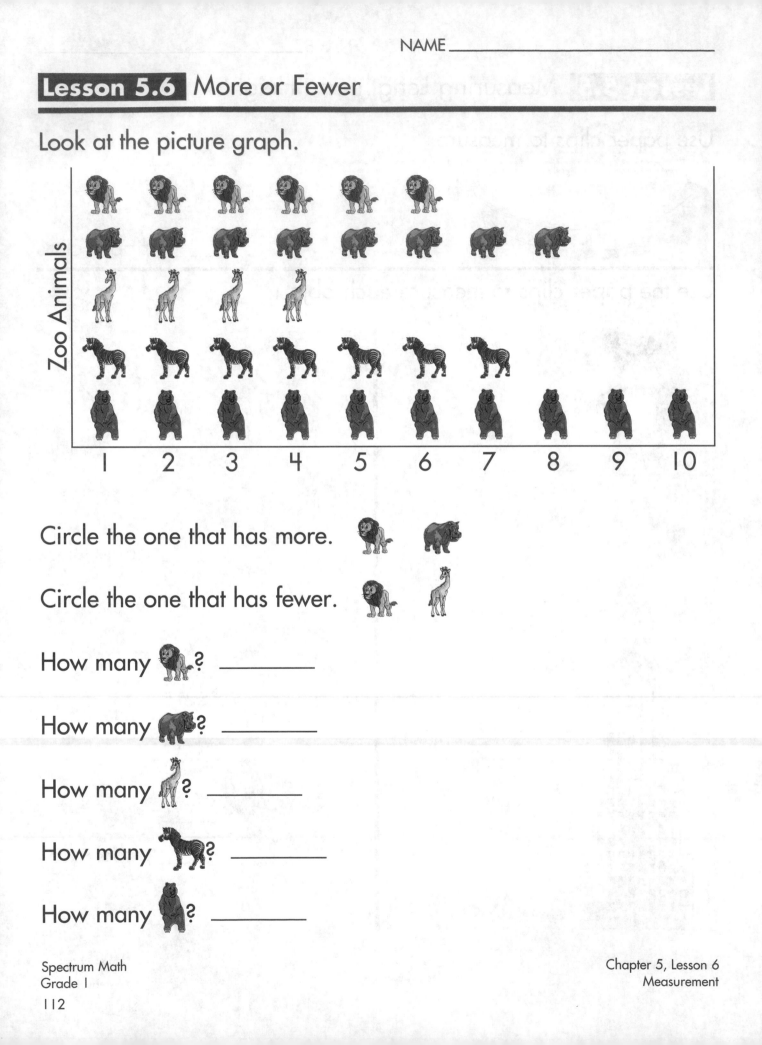

Circle the one that has more.

Circle the one that has fewer.

How many 🦁? _____

How many 🦛? _____

How many 🦒? _____

How many 🦓? _____

How many 🐻? _____

Lesson 5.7 Greater Than, Less Than, and Equal To

Look at the picture graph.

Circle the object that is greater than ⬜.

Circle the object that is less than 🥄.

Circle the object that is equal to 🍴.

Circle the object that is equal to 🍽.

Fill in the _____ with *greater than*, *less than*, or *equal to*.

☕ is ___less than___ 🍴.

🥄 is _____ ⬜.

⬜ is _____ 🍽.

🍴 is _____ 🍽.

Lesson 5.8 Collecting Data

Make a food chart for one day. Show what you ate.

Fruit

Vegetable

Meat/Eggs/Fish

Bread/Cereal

Other Foods

Breakfast	
Lunch	
Dinner	
Snacks	

Use your food chart.

How many of each did you eat?

Fruit _____   Bread/Cereal _____

Vegetable _____   Other Foods _____

Meat/Eggs/Fish _____

What food did you eat the most? _____

At which meal did you eat the most? _____

What is your favorite food? _____

Lesson 5.8 Collecting Data

Make a pet chart. Ask 20 people if they have a pet.
Use tally marks to show what kind.

Tally Marks
I = 1
II = 2
III = 3
IIII = 4
IIII = 5

				Other	None

Use your pet chart. Write the number.

How many people have 🐕? _____

How many people have 🐈? _____

How many people have 🐦? _____

How many people have 🐟? _____

How many people do not have a pet? _____

How many people have a pet that is not on the chart? _____

Complete.

Which pet is the favorite? _____

Which pet is the least favorite? _____

Lesson 5.8 Collecting Data

Make a fruit chart. Ask 20 people if they have a favorite fruit.

Use tally marks to show what kind.

Tally Marks
I = 1
II = 2
III = 3
IIII = 4
IIII = 5

🍎	🍌	🍑	🍇	Other	None

Use your fruit chart. Write the number.

How many people like 🍎? _____

How many people like 🍌? _____

How many people like 🍑? _____

How many people like 🍇? _____

How many people like a fruit that is not on the chart? _____

How many people do not like fruit? _____

Complete.

Which is the favorite fruit? _____

Which is the least favorite fruit? _____

How many more people chose the
favorite fruit than chose the least favorite fruit? _____

Check What You Learned

Measurement

Write the time for each clock.

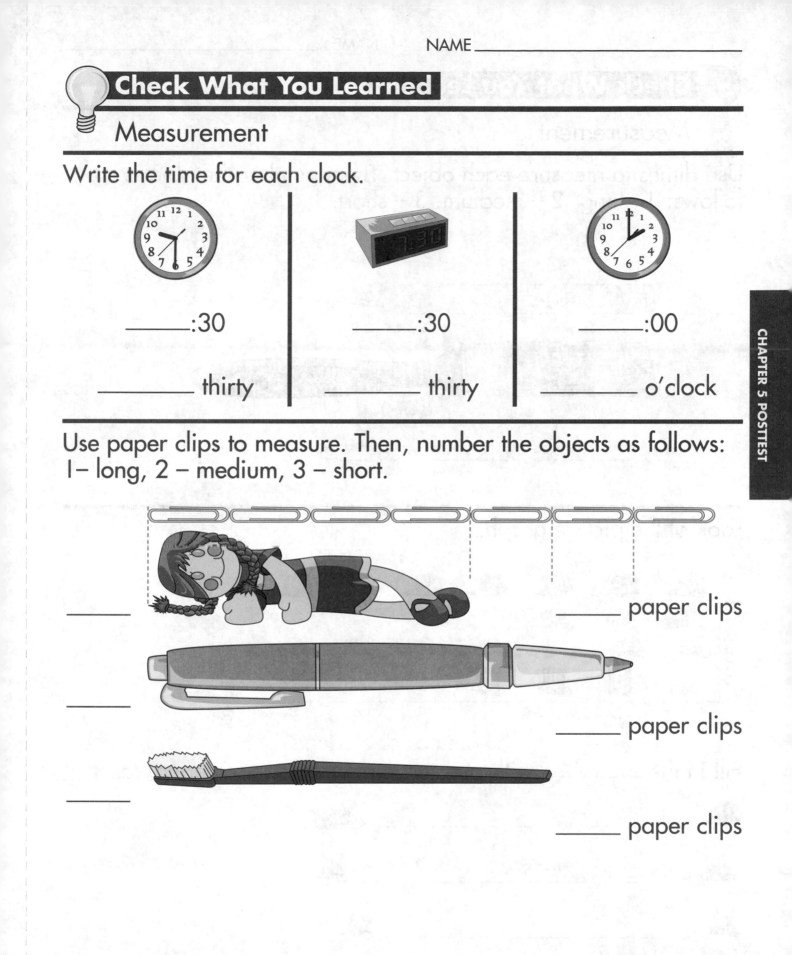

_____:30

_____ thirty

_____:30

_____ thirty

_____:00

_____ o'clock

Use paper clips to measure. Then, number the objects as follows:
1– long, 2 – medium, 3 – short.

_____

_____ paper clips

_____ paper clips

_____ paper clips

Check What You Learned

Measurement

Use dimes to measure each object. Then, number the objects as follows: 1– long, 2 – medium, 3 – short.

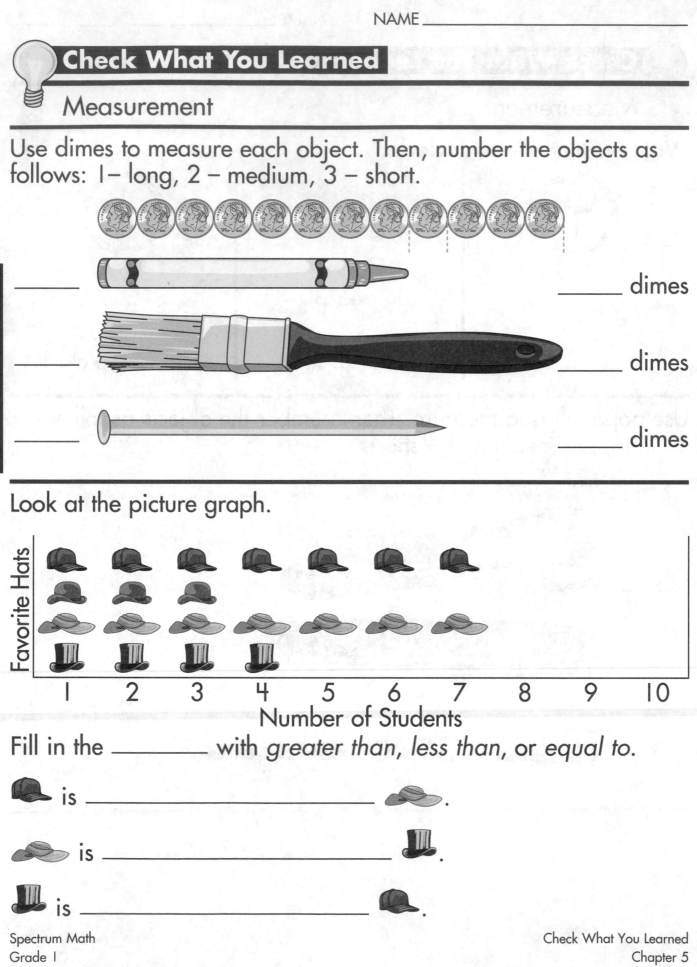

_____ _____ dimes

_____ _____ dimes

_____ _____ dimes

Look at the picture graph.

Fill in the _____ with *greater than*, *less than*, or *equal to*.

_____ is _____ _____.

_____ is _____ _____.

_____ is _____ _____.

Check What You Know

Geometry

Write the name of each shape.

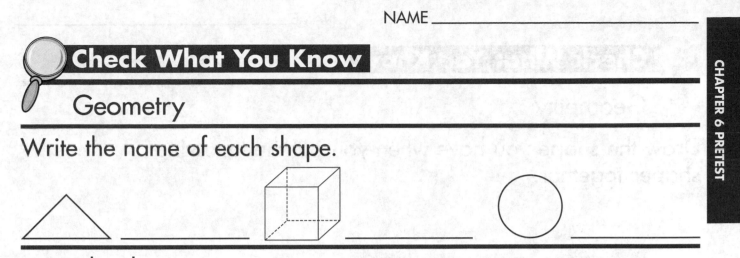

_____ _____ _____

Draw the shape.

Circle
It is a closed curve.

Rectangle
It has 4 sides.

Triangle
It has 3 angles.

Write the name of the shape. Then, draw the shape.

_____

_____

NAME _____

Check What You Know

Geometry

Draw the shape you have when you put the following shapes together.

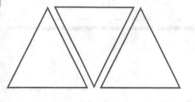

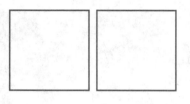

Draw lines to show how you and a friend can equally share this piece of gum.	Draw a line to show how you and a friend can equally share this pancake.	There are _____ equal parts. _____ of the parts is shaded. _____ of the shape is shaded.
		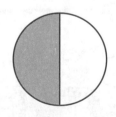

Lesson 6.1 Identifying Shapes

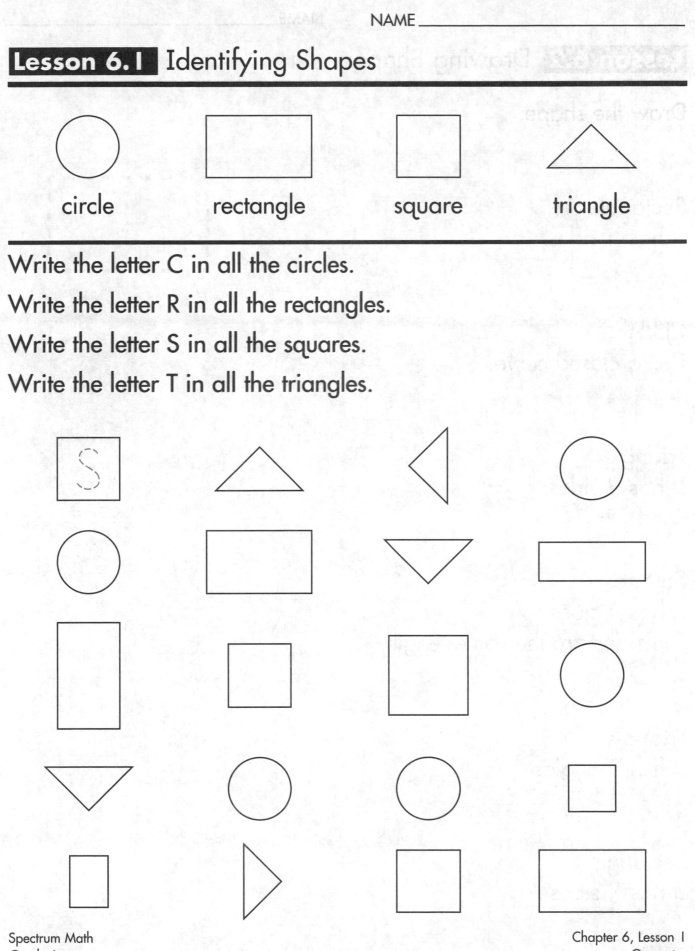

circle

rectangle

square

triangle

Write the letter C in all the circles.

Write the letter R in all the rectangles.

Write the letter S in all the squares.

Write the letter T in all the triangles.

Lesson 6.2 Drawing Shapes

Draw the shape.

Rectangle
It has 4 sides.

Circle
It is a closed curve.

Triangle
It has 3 sides.

Square
It has 4 sides.
The sides are the same length.

Triangle
It has 3 angles.

Rectangle
It has 4 sides.

Lesson 6.3 Finding Shapes

Write the name of each shape. Then, draw the shape.

circle

Lesson 6.3 Finding Shapes

Write the name of each shape. Then, draw the shape.

triangle

Lesson 6.4 Composing 2-D Shapes

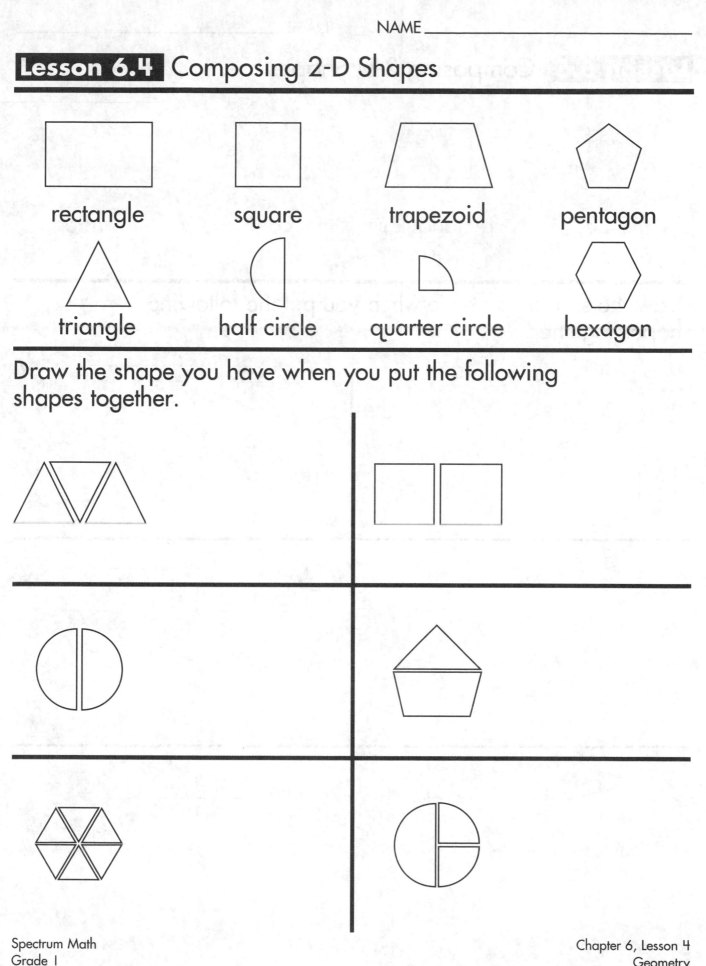

rectangle   square   trapezoid   pentagon

triangle   half circle   quarter circle   hexagon

Draw the shape you have when you put the following shapes together.

Lesson 6.5 Composing 3-D Shapes

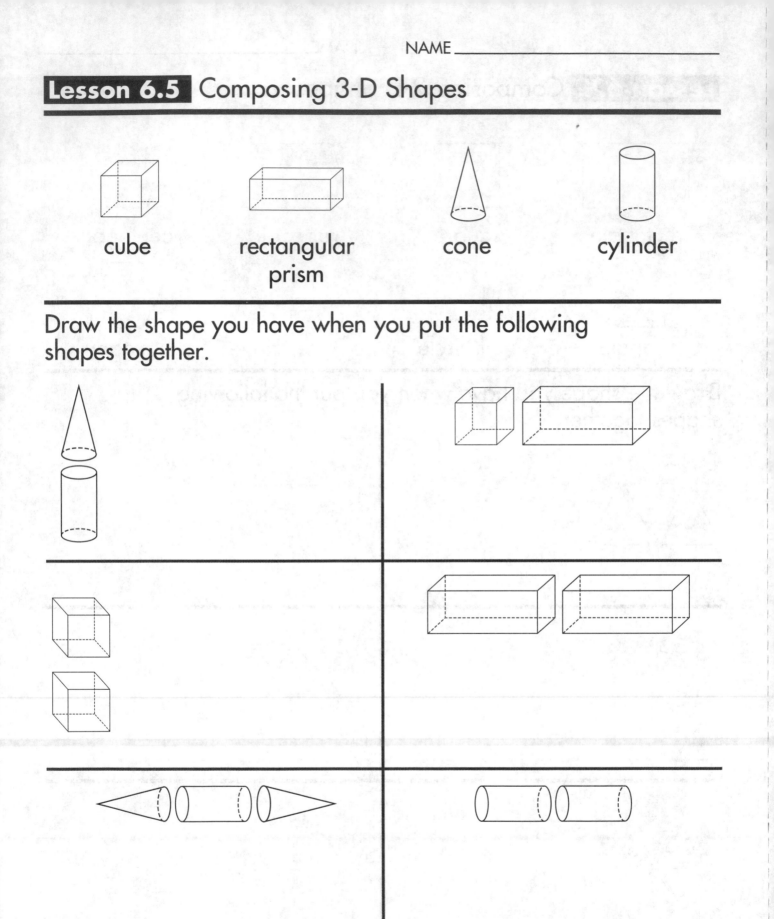

cube   rectangular prism   cone   cylinder

Draw the shape you have when you put the following shapes together.

Lesson 6.6 Partitioning Shapes

A shape can be divided into equal pieces. It can be divided into two equal pieces, three equal pieces, or four equal pieces.

Draw lines to show how you and a friend can equally share each item.

Draw lines to show how you and 2 friends can equally share each item.

Draw lines to show how you and 3 friends can equally share each item.

Lesson 6.7 One-Half and One-Fourth

One-half of the whole is shaded.

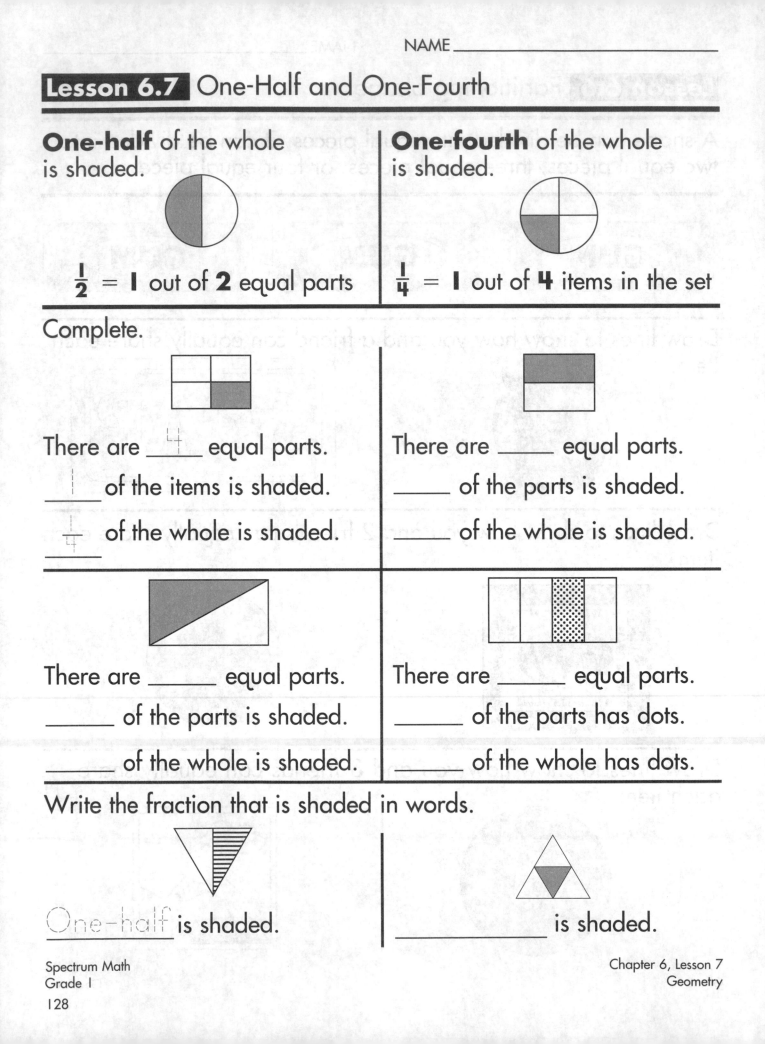

$\frac{1}{2}$ = **1** out of **2** equal parts

One-fourth of the whole is shaded.

$\frac{1}{4}$ = **1** out of **4** items in the set

Complete.

There are __4__ equal parts.

__1__ of the items is shaded.

$\frac{1}{4}$ of the whole is shaded.

There are _____ equal parts.

_____ of the parts is shaded.

_____ of the whole is shaded.

There are _____ equal parts.

_____ of the parts is shaded.

_____ of the whole is shaded.

There are _____ equal parts.

_____ of the parts has dots.

_____ of the whole has dots.

Write the fraction that is shaded in words.

One-half is shaded.

_____ is shaded.

Check What You Learned

Geometry

Write the name of each shape.

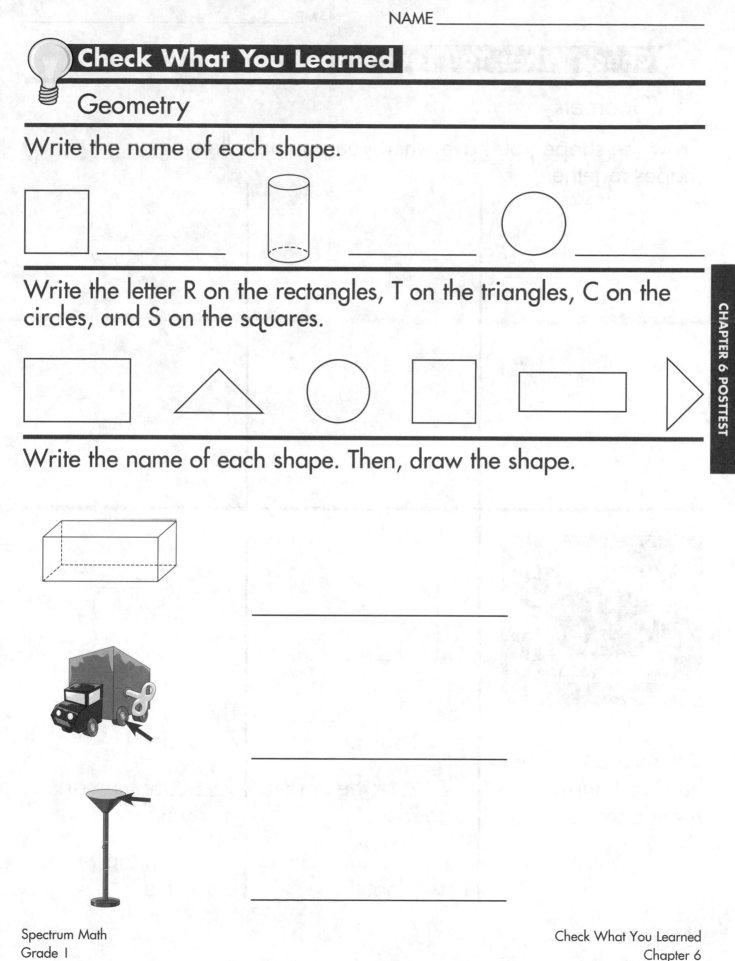

_____   _____   _____

Write the letter R on the rectangles, T on the triangles, C on the circles, and S on the squares.

Write the name of each shape. Then, draw the shape.

_____

_____

_____

CHAPTER 6 POSTTEST

Check What You Learned

Geometry

Draw the shape you have when you put the following shapes together.

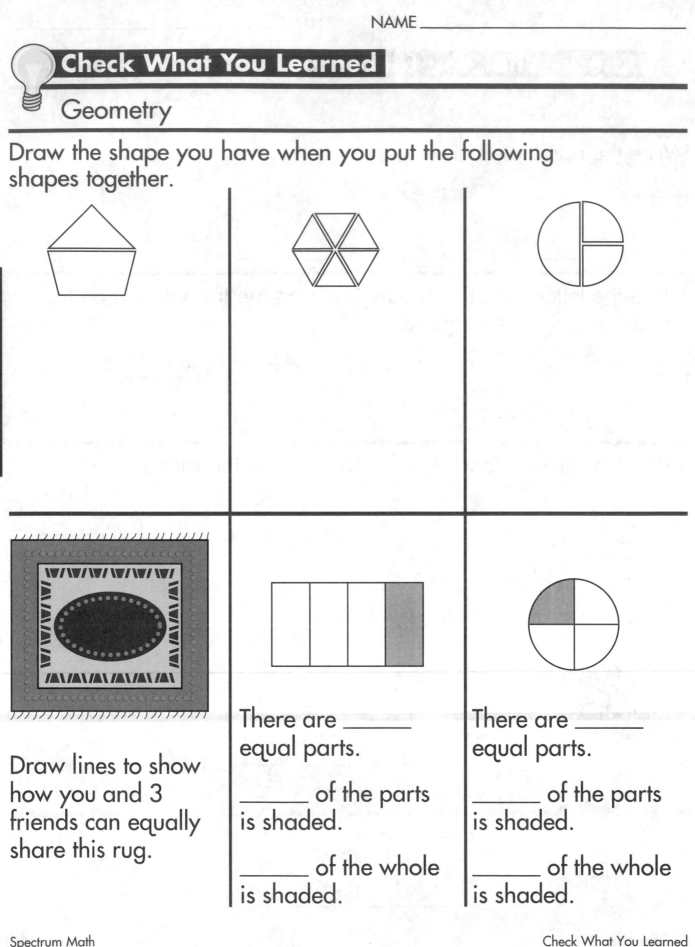

Draw lines to show how you and 3 friends can equally share this rug.

There are _____ equal parts.

_____ of the parts is shaded.

_____ of the whole is shaded.

There are _____ equal parts.

_____ of the parts is shaded.

_____ of the whole is shaded.

Final Test Chapters 1–6

Add.

5 +3	8 +4	9 +2	6 +4	7 +1	3 +2
7 +8	8 +9	4 +1	4 +5	8 +8	2 +1
15 +5	6 +8	7 +5	3 +3	1 +3	9 +0
0 +1	9 +9	7 +7	6 +7	1 +1	2 +5
5 +5	7 +0	12 +7	9 +8	6 +9	0 +0
6 +3	2 +2	8 +2	9 +7	4 +4	10 +9
6 +6	8 +5	1 +5	5 +0	6 +1	0 +8

Final Test Chapters 1-6

Subtract.

18 − 9	12 − 4	11 − 2	10 − 4	8 − 7	5 − 2
15 − 8	17 − 9	9 − 7	19 − 4	13 − 5	3 − 1
9 − 5	14 − 8	12 − 5	6 − 3	4 − 3	9 − 0
1 − 1	15 − 6	14 − 7	13 − 7	2 − 1	7 − 5
15 − 9	7 − 0	19 − 6	17 − 8	5 − 5	3 − 0
6 − 3	9 − 7	10 − 2	5 − 1	8 − 4	14 − 5
12 − 6	16 − 8	6 − 5	20 − 3	7 − 1	8 − 8

Final Test Chapters 1–6

SHOW YOUR WORK

Solve each problem.

I have 15 ⚾.

I find 5 more ⚾.

How many ⚾ do I have? _____

There are 7 🐕.

4 more 🐕 come.

How many 🐕 are there in all? _____

There are 8 🚚.

There are 2 🚂.

What is 8 plus 2? _____

Joseph buys 🍎 for 7¢.

He buys 🍑 for 9¢.

How much money did he spend? _____ ¢

Imala has 5 ✏.

She has 3 🖊.

What is 5 plus 3? _____

There are 6 🦛.

6 more 🦛 come.

What is 6 + 6? _____

Final Test Chapters 1–6

Solve each problem.

Pamela has 10¢.

She buys ✐ for 8¢.

How much money does she have left? _____ ¢

There are 17 🐦.

9 🐦 fly away.

What is 17 minus 9? _____

Myron wants 18 🚓.

He has 9 🚓.

How many more 🚓 does he want? _____

Omar has 19 ✏.

Lulu has 1 ✏.

How many more pencils does Omar have? _____

There are 7 🐿.

3 🐿 run away.

How many 🐿 are left? _____

Kiru has 15 ✏.

She gives 6 ✏ away.

How many ✏ does she have left? _____

Spectrum Math
Grade 1
134

CHAPTERS 1–6 FINAL TEST

Final Test
Chapters 1–6

Final Test Chapters 1–6

Count forward. Write the missing numbers.

1				5					10
11		13				17		19	
	22		24		26				
		33					38		40
	42			45		47			50
		53	54					59	
61	62				66				
			74			77			80
81		83					88		
	92			95		97			100
101					106			109	
111		113					118		

Final Test Chapters 1–6

Write <, >, or = to make the following statements true.

35 ☐ 36   64 ☐ 44   13 ☐ 23

73 ☐ 37   98 ☐ 89   41 ☐ 14

Complete.

_____ tens _____ ones = _____

_____ tens _____ ones = _____

_____ tens _____ ones = _____

_____ ten _____ ones = _____

Complete.

8 tens and 7 ones = _____   8 tens and 9 ones = _____

7 tens and 5 ones = _____   3 tens and 9 ones = _____

5 tens and 4 ones = _____   0 tens and 7 ones = _____

4 tens and 8 ones = _____   2 tens and 5 ones = _____

3 tens and 1 one = _____   7 tens and 2 ones = _____

Spectrum Math
Grade 1
136

Final Test
Chapters 1–6

CHAPTERS 1–6 FINAL TEST

Final Test Chapters 1–6

Use dimes to measure each object.

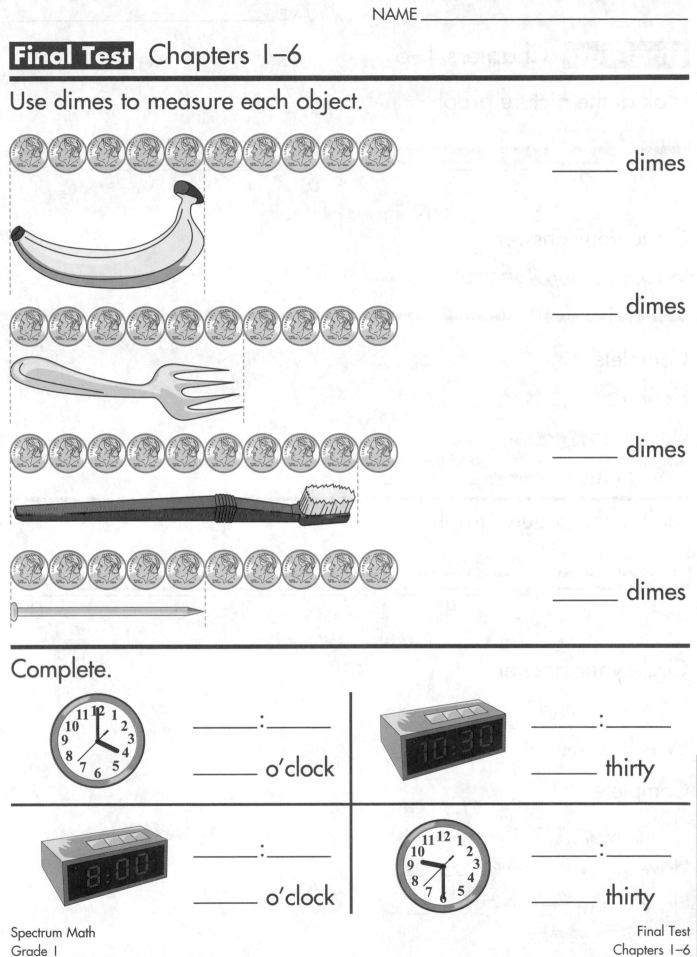

_____ dimes

_____ dimes

_____ dimes

_____ dimes

Complete.

_____ : _____
_____ o'clock

_____ : _____
_____ thirty

_____ : _____
_____ o'clock

_____ : _____
_____ thirty

Final Test Chapters 1-6

Look at the picture graph.

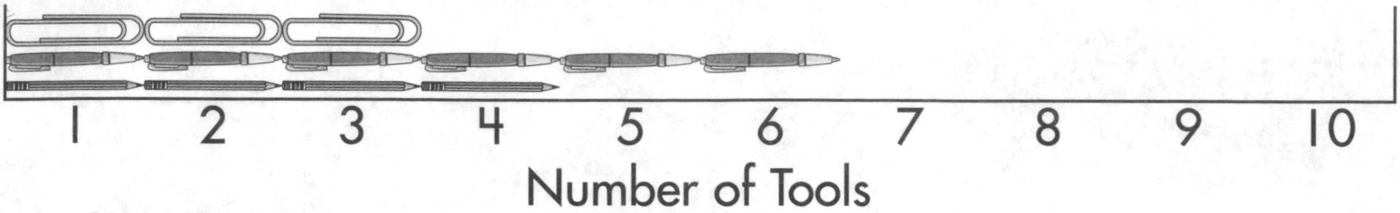

| 1 | 2 | 3 | 4 | 5 | 6 | 7 | 8 | 9 | 10 |

Number of Tools

Circle your answer.

Which is more? 📎 ✏️

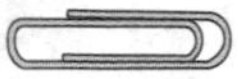

Which is fewer? ✏️ 🖊️

Complete.

How many 📎? _____

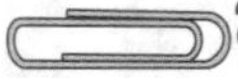

How many 🖊️? _____

How many ✏️? _____

Look at the picture graph.

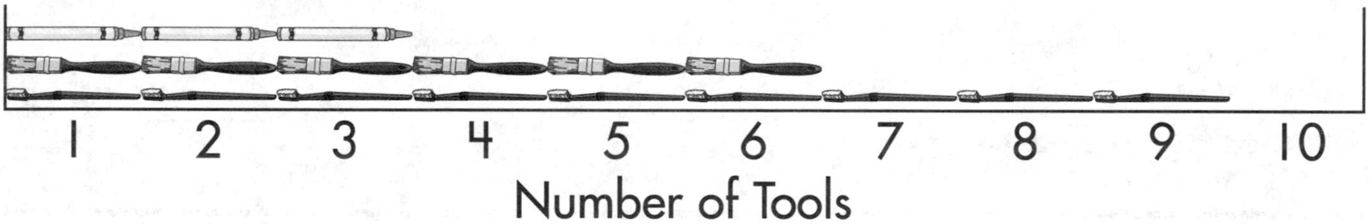

| 1 | 2 | 3 | 4 | 5 | 6 | 7 | 8 | 9 | 10 |

Number of Tools

Circle your answer.

Which is more? ✏️ 🖌️

Which is fewer? 🖌️ ✏️

Complete.

How many ✏️? _____

How many 🖌️? _____

How many ✏️? _____

Final Test Chapters 1–6

Draw the shape.

triangle   cube   circle

Draw the shape you have when you put the following shapes together.

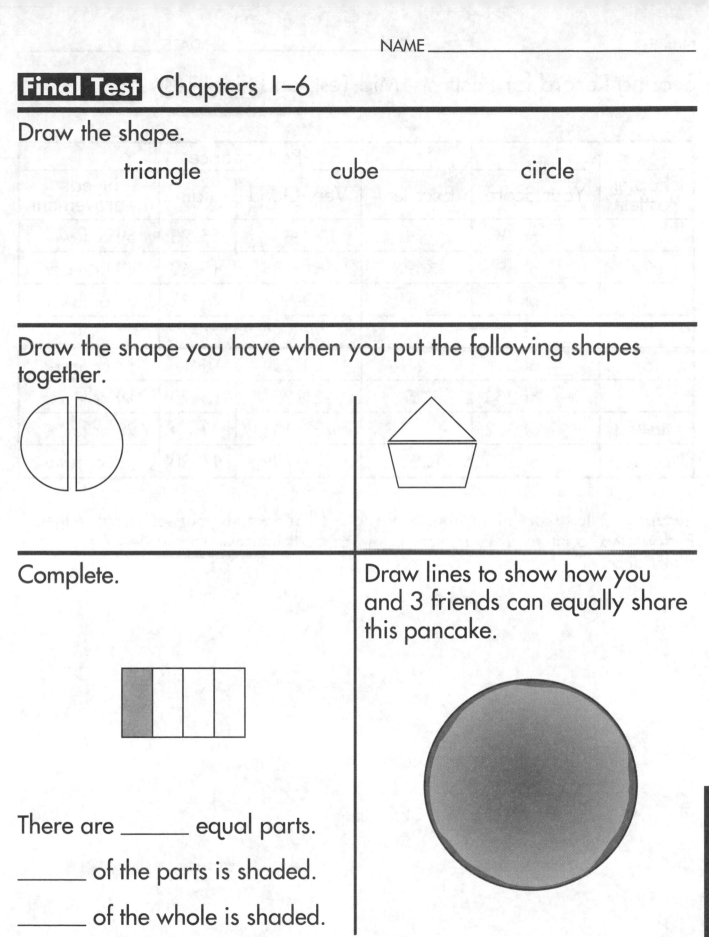

Complete.

There are _____ equal parts.

_____ of the parts is shaded.

_____ of the whole is shaded.

Draw lines to show how you and 3 friends can equally share this pancake.

Scoring Record for Posttests, Mid-Test, and Final Test

Chapter Posttest	Your Score	Performance			
		Excellent	Very Good	Fair	Needs Improvement
1	____ of 84	84	74–83	55–73	54 or fewer
2	____ of 69	69	61–68	45–60	44 or fewer
3	____ of 41	41	33–40	26–32	28 or fewer
4	____ of 30	30	24–29	21–23	20 or fewer
5	____ of 21	21	18–20	14–17	13 or fewer
6	____ of 25	25	21–24	15–20	14 or fewer
Mid-Test	____ of 162	162	143–161	100–142	99 or fewer
Final Test	____ of 240	240	209–239	147–208	146 or fewer

Record your test score in the Your Score column. See where your score falls in the Performance columns. If your score is fair or needs improvement, review the chapter material again.

Chapter 1

Pretest, page 5

6	5	2	6	6	5
4	3	3	4	6	3
6	6	4			
4	6	6			
5	2	2	2	2	3
3	2	1	1	1	5
1	4	1			
3	1	0			

Pretest, page 6

6
3
2
3

Pretest, page 7

10	9	10	8	8	7
8	9	9	10	10	7
10	5	7	9	10	8
5	2	6	2	6	9
1	7	0	4	7	3
9	1	4	8	7	1

Pretest, page 8

9
3
3¢
7
5
10¢

Lesson 1.1, page 9

2	3
2	3
	3
	3
1	2
1	2
1	2
1	2
3	0
3	0
3	
3	

Lesson 1.2, page 10

1	0
1	0
2	1
2	1
2	0
2	0
0	1
0	1

Lesson 1.3, page 11

5	4
5	4
5	
5	
4	5
4	5

4	5
4	5
4	5
4	5
4	5

6	3
6	3
4	1
4	1

5 3 4 0 2 1

Lesson 1.4, page 12

Lesson 1.7, page 15

6	6
6	6
6	6
6	6
6	6
6	6
6	
6	

6 6 5 6 6 5
5 6 6
6 6 4

5 5 3 2	6 6 1 5
4	6
4	3
1	
3	
3 3 2 1	4 4 0 4
4 2	5 5 1 4

Lesson 1.5, page 13

Lesson 1.7, page 16

3	0
3	0
2	4
2	4
5	3
5	3
1	1
1	1

6 6 4 2	2 1
2	5
2	5
2	0
0	5
5 5 3 2	6 6 6 0
3	1
3	1 1 0
0	1 1 0
3	0

Lesson 1.6, page 14

Lesson 1.8, page 17

2	5
2	5

3
4
2
3

Grade 1 Answers

5
5

Lesson 1.8, page 18

6
6
6
2
2
4

Lesson 1.8, page 19

2
5
1
1
4
2

Lesson 1.9, page 20

7	7
7	7
7	7
7	7
7	7
7	7
7	7
7	7

7   7   7   7   7   7

Lesson 1.10, page 21

4	6
4	6

2	7
2	7
1	3
1	3
5	0
5	0

Lesson 1.11, page 22

8	8
8	8
8	8
8	8
8	8
8	8
8	
8	

8   8   8   8   8   8

Lesson 1.12, page 23

6	4
6	4
2	1
2	1
7	0
7	0
5	3
5	3

Lesson 1.13, page 24

9	9
9	9
9	9

9		9
9		9
9		9
9		9
9		9
9		9
9		9

9	9	9	9	9	9

Lesson 1.14, page 25

2		6
2		6
4		8
4		8
7		5
7		5

3	0	9	1

Lesson 1.15, page 26

10		10
10		10
10		10
10		10
10		10
10		10
10		10
10		10

10	10	10	10	10	10

Lesson 1.16, page 27

4		5
4		5

7		2
7		2
9		0
9		0
8		1
8		1
3		6
3		6

Lesson 1.17, page 28

9 9 5 4		10 10 7 3
7		9
7		9
2		3
5		6
8 8 7 1		10 5
7 7 3 4		8 8 6 2

Lesson 1.17, page 29

10 10 4 6		8 4
9		10
9		10
7		8
2		2
8 8 3 5		7 7 6 1
9 9 8 1		7 7 7 0

Lesson 1.18, page 30

8	9	9	10	6	7
9	7	10	10	9	10
8	5	7	8	10	9

Grade 1 Answers

7	7	10	10	4	9
9	10	7	3	10	8
9	6	7	9	10	3

Lesson 1.18, page 31

10
9
8
7
10

Lesson 1.19, page 32

6	1	6	4	9	0
2	8	4	3	4	0
3	0	5	3	8	7
5	1	0	6	4	10
5	1	7	7	9	2
2	2	3	7	4	3

Lesson 1.19, page 33

3
7
4
5
4

Lesson 1.20, page 34

7¢	10¢
8¢	9¢
10¢	5¢
8¢	6¢

Lesson 1.21, page 35

7¢
10¢
8¢
5¢
1¢
9¢

Lesson 1.21, page 36

3¢
8¢
10¢
8¢
0¢
7¢

Lesson 1.22, page 37

9
9
8
8
8
6
9
10
7

Lesson 1.23, page 38

4	4
7	7
5	5
6	6

4	4
6	6
2	2
1	1
3	3

Lesson 1.24, page 39

	4	6	7
2	3		10
	6	8	9
	8		2
4	5	6	7

Posttest, page 40

5	6	5	6	3	4
6	4	4	1	6	5
4	3	5	2	6	6
3	5	0	3	1	6
2	2	2	3	0	1
3	1	4	1	4	0

Posttest, page 41

5
3
3
6
1
4

Posttest, page 42

9	7	8	10	10	9
9	10	8	7	8	10

9	8	7	10	8	7
2	10	4	4	0	3
8	8	5	3	5	5
1	0	3	8	6	7

Posttest, page 43

6
10¢
8
7
2¢
8¢

Chapter 2
Pretest, page 44

3 tens 6 ones = 36
6 tens 2 ones = 62
4 tens 1 one = 41
1 ten 2 ones = 12

96	78
84	49
63	16
57	34
20	81

Pretest, page 45

25, 28, 30, 31
73, 77, 80, 84
102, 106, 109
50, 51, 52, 55
113, 114, 115, 118, 119, 120
30, 50, 90, 100, 110

Grade 1 Answers

40 > 37	77 = 77	18 < 70
55 > 35	38 > 27	9 < 34
22 < 44	85 < 88	71 < 75
14 < 32	30 > 20	65 < 76
59 > 39	43 < 76	29 > 19
52 > 21	36 > 26	64 > 8

Lesson 2.1, page 46

1 ten 0 ones = 10
1 ten 1 one = 11
1 ten 2 ones = 12
1 ten 3 ones = 13
1 ten 4 ones = 14

Lesson 2.2, page 47

1 ten 5 ones = 15
1 ten 6 ones = 16
1 ten 7 ones = 17
1 ten 8 ones = 18
1 ten 9 ones = 19

Lesson 2.3, page 48

2 tens 0 ones = 20
2 tens 1 one = 21
2 tens 2 ones = 22
2 tens 3 ones = 23
2 tens 4 ones = 24

Lesson 2.4, page 49

2 tens 5 ones = 25
2 tens 6 ones = 26
2 tens 7 ones = 27
2 tens 8 ones = 28
2 tens 9 ones = 29

Lesson 2.5, page 50

3 tens 4 ones = 34
4 tens 2 ones = 42
3 tens 0 ones = 30
4 tens 3 ones = 43

44	39
36	45
41	37
38	40
46	33

Lesson 2.6, page 51

5 tens 1 one = 51
6 tens 3 ones = 63
5 tens 4 ones = 54
6 tens 2 ones = 62

60	69
52	64
67	55
53	66
58	57

Lesson 2.7, page 52

76	98
83	80
71	75
87	99
94	91
92	86
79	70
88	82

Grade 1 Answers

Lesson 2.8, page 53

1	2	3	4	5	6	7	8	9	10
11	12	13	14	15	16	17	18	19	20
21	22	23	24	25	26	27	28	29	30
31	32	33	34	35	36	37	38	39	40
41	42	43	44	45	46	47	48	49	50
51	52	53	54	55	56	57	58	59	60
61	62	63	64	65	66	67	68	69	70
71	72	73	74	75	76	77	78	79	80
81	82	83	84	85	86	87	88	89	90
91	92	93	94	95	96	97	98	99	100
101	102	103	104	105	106	107	108	109	110
111	112	113	114	115	116	117	118	119	120

Lesson 2.9, page 54

94, 97, 100, 101
66, 69, 72, 76
102, 105, 107, 110
5, 20, 40, 60
10, 40, 60, 90, 100, 110, 120
78, 75, 71, 68
83, 80, 76, 75
20, 14, 10, 4
115, 100, 85, 80
65, 50, 30, 20
110, 100, 80, 50, 40, 20

Lesson 2.10, page 55

16 < 22	78 > 38	86 < 88
37 > 18	45 = 45	15 < 26
51 < 56	73 < 99	92 = 92
70 = 70	24 < 25	19 > 11
35 < 74	40 > 30	48 < 89
81 > 43	13 = 13	36 > 34
12 < 20	33 < 42	63 = 63
62 > 41	21 > 17	71 > 61

Lesson 2.10, page 56

77 < 87	97 < 98	6 < 49
90 > 80	4 < 27	69 > 58
79 > 5	46 < 75	1 < 10
53 > 32	94 > 82	50 < 93
64 = 64	67 > 29	95 > 3
84 < 96	60 > 39	15 > 11
23 > 9	55 < 72	63 = 63
57 < 85	2 < 68	59 < 83
52 > 31	91 > 8	47 > 37
47 = 47	66 < 83	50 = 50
28 > 7	14 < 59	21 < 31
44 < 54	76 > 65	35 > 23

Posttest, page 57

2 tens 4 ones = 24
3 tens 3 ones = 33
6 tens 0 ones = 60
1 ten 5 ones = 15

48	81
73	58
95	39
62	27
56	11

Posttest, page 58

48, 52, 53, 56
95, 98, 99, 101, 104
111, 114, 115, 116, 118, 120
20, 35, 50, 65

Grade 1 Answers

70, 90, 95, 100, 115, 120
50, 60, 70, 110

73 > 60	61 > 51	16 < 68
81 > 13	90 > 17	54 > 5
44 > 33	67 < 95	41 < 69
45 = 45	93 = 93	78 < 79
57 > 56	72 > 62	74 > 25
86 < 97	46 < 48	84 > 3

Mid-Test

Page 59

10 10 7 3	9 9 7 2
6 6 4 2	7 7 5 2
3 tens 6 ones = 36	5 tens 5 ones = 55
4 tens 0 ones = 40	9 tens 7 ones = 97

Page 60

66 > 49	58 = 58	6 < 68
63 > 53	42 < 50	87 < 89
12 < 25	68 > 54	24 < 54
92 > 82	10 < 91	23 > 15
28 < 58	11 < 31	98 > 94

87, 89, 92, 95
107, 108, 112, 113
59, 62, 65, 66
25, 40, 60, 75
20, 30, 60, 80, 100, 110, 120

Page 61

9	5	9	8	9	10
9	7	10	5	6	4

10	9	6	7	8	5
1	6	7	10	8	7
10	6	8	5	8	2
0	3	6	5	4	7
8	8	10	9	9	10

Page 62

2	1	8	3	2	2
3	1	4	0	2	1
6	2	0	1	4	6
6	3	3	3	0	7
5	0	8	8	2	9
2	3	0	2	0	5
5	10	7	4	1	0

Page 63

9¢
8
6
5¢
10¢
5

Page 64

4¢
2
5
2¢
6
1¢

Grade 1 Answers

Chapter 3

Pretest, page 65

11	18	15	14	13	12
17	16	16	13	12	11
15	13	14	19	19	20

8	4	9	11	6	7
12	7	9	9	8	6
3	8	8	7	12	6

Pretest, page 66

17
7
11
14
7

Lesson 3.1, page 67

11	11
11	11
11	11
11	11

11	11	11	11	11	11

Lesson 3.2, page 68

3	8
6	5
7	4
9	2

8	5	2	3	7	11

Lesson 3.3, page 69

12	12
12	12
12	12

12	12	12	12	12	12
12	12	12			
12	12	12			

Lesson 3.4, page 70

5	7
6	4
3	9

8	9	4	5	6	7
3	4	6			
5	9	8			

Lesson 3.5, page 71

13	13
13	13
13	13

13	13	13	13	13	13
13	13	13			
13	13	13			

Lesson 3.6, page 72

4	9
7	13
5	8

4	5	8	6	13	7
6	5	9			
8	4	7			

Lesson 3.7, page 73

14		14
14		14
14		14

14	14	14	14	14	14
14	14	14			

Lesson 3.8, page 74

8	6				
9	5				
7	14				
14	7	6	5	8	9
7	5	8			
6	12	11			

Lesson 3.9, page 75

14	14	11	3
15	15		
0	15		
13	13	12	1
15	15	12	3

Lesson 3.10, page 76

15	15				
15	14	15	13	14	13

15	13	15	14	14	13
6	9				
6	7	9	5	8	6
8	9	9	4	7	6

Lesson 3.10, page 77

6
15
15
8
9

Lesson 3.11, page 78

17	17	14	3
18	18		
16	2		
19	19	18	1
20	20		
4	16		

Lesson 3.12, page 79

16	16				
14	16	15	16	14	15
15	14	16	14	14	15
7	9				
8	8	5	6	7	9
9	6	7	9	7	8

Lesson 3.12, page 80

16

8
9
16
16

Lesson 3.13, page 81

14,14; 15,15; 14, 14; 17, 17; 11,
11; 12, 12; 15, 15;
14, 14; 13, 13

Lesson 3.14, page 82

17	18				
16	17	14	15	18	14
15	14	17	15	16	15
8	9	9			
7	8	7	9	9	9
9	8	7	8	8	9

Lesson 3.14, page 83

8
18
17
9
9

Lesson 3.15, page 84

13, 13; 13, 13; 12, 12; 11, 11;
12, 12; 11, 11; 12, 12;
11, 11; 12, 12

Lesson 3.16, page 85

12; 19; 10; 10; 17; 15; 18; 17;
16

Posttest, page 86

15	17	13	19	11	14
12	13	16	20	12	18
12	15	13	11	15	14
9	8	13	8	7	8
9	7	6	8	4	9
4	7	9	8	4	11

Posttest, page 87

12
13
9
15
16

Chapter 4

Pretest, page 88

21	20	15	21	25
24	59	72	31	48
30	0	70	30	10
30	20	30	30	20
17	20	19	18	17
6	9	10	15	15

Lesson 4.1, page 89

17	25	32	26	17
46	28	32	49	15
68	59	89	45	88

Lesson 4.1, page 90

69	47	38	79	65
49	25	39	23	26

36	88	49	61	55
23	68	45	60	44
31	24	50	19	92
94	40	72	29	44

Lesson 4.2, page 91

25	39	43	41	67
43	69	57	61	90
85	90	95	92	92
38	92	60	79	85
57	31	79	96	95

Lesson 4.3, page 92

33; 24; 38; 33; 76; 64

Lesson 4.4, page 93

40	20
10	10
10	20

Lesson 4.4, page 94

40	30
70	10
20	30
80	0
50	60

Lesson 4.5, page 95

17	16	25	35	33	44
58	76	65	27	84	100
93	34	85	16	54	73
10	10	20	10	50	20
10	40	0	30	50	30

0	10	60	20	10	60

Lesson 4.5, page 96

20; 25; 30; 46; 50

Lesson 4.6, page 97

18	19	9	20	6
7	11	17	8	6
10	17	16	19	20

Lesson 4.6, page 98

17; 18; 12; 20; 20

Posttest, page 99

16	20	18	18	19
35	47	63	30	78
40	0	10	10	70
20	10	50	50	0
16	20	16	17	14
4	7	7	14	16

Chapter 5

Pretest, page 100

4:00, 4 o'clock; 3:30,
3 thirty; 10:30, 10 thirty
2, 4 paperclips
3, 3 paperclips
1, 5 paperclips

Pretest, page 101

1, 7 dimes
3, 5 dimes

2, 6 dimes

Lesson 5.1, page 102

4:00 4 o'clock	9:00 9 o'clock
3:00 3 o'clock	7:00 7 o'clock
12:00 12 o'clock	2:00 2 o'clock
1:00 1 o'clock	6:00 6 o'clock

Lesson 5.1, page 103

6:00	7:00
8:00	2:00

Lesson 5.2, page 104

1:30 1 thirty	5:30 5 thirty
7:30 7 thirty	10:30 10 thirty
12:30 12 thirty	2:30 2 thirty
6:30 6 thirty	9:30 9 thirty

Lesson 5.2, page 105

4:30	11:30
8:30	3:30

Lesson 5.3, page 106

3	1	2	3	2	1
2	3	1	3	1	2
	2		3	1	2
	3				
	1				

Lesson 5.3, page 107

2	1	3	2	3	1
2	3	1	3	1	2
1	2	3	3	1	2

Lesson 5.4, page 108

Lesson 5.4, page 109

Grade 1 Answers

Lesson 5.5, page 110

7	8
4	5
6	
5	

Lesson 5.5, page 111

5	5
3	4
6	

Lesson 5.6, page 112

6
8
4
7
10

Lesson 5.7, page 113

less than
greater than

equal to
greater than

Lesson 5.8, page 114

Answers will vary.

Lesson 5.8, page 115

Answers will vary.

Lesson 5.8, page 116

Answers will vary.

Posttest, page 117

9:30	7:30	2:00
9 thirty	7 thirty	2 o'clock

3, 4 paper clips
1, 6 paper clips
2, 5 paper clips

Posttest, page 118

3, 8 dimes
1, 12 dimes
2, 9 dimes
equal to; greater than; less than

Chapter 6

Pretest, page 119

triangle   cube   circle

Grade 1 Answers

cone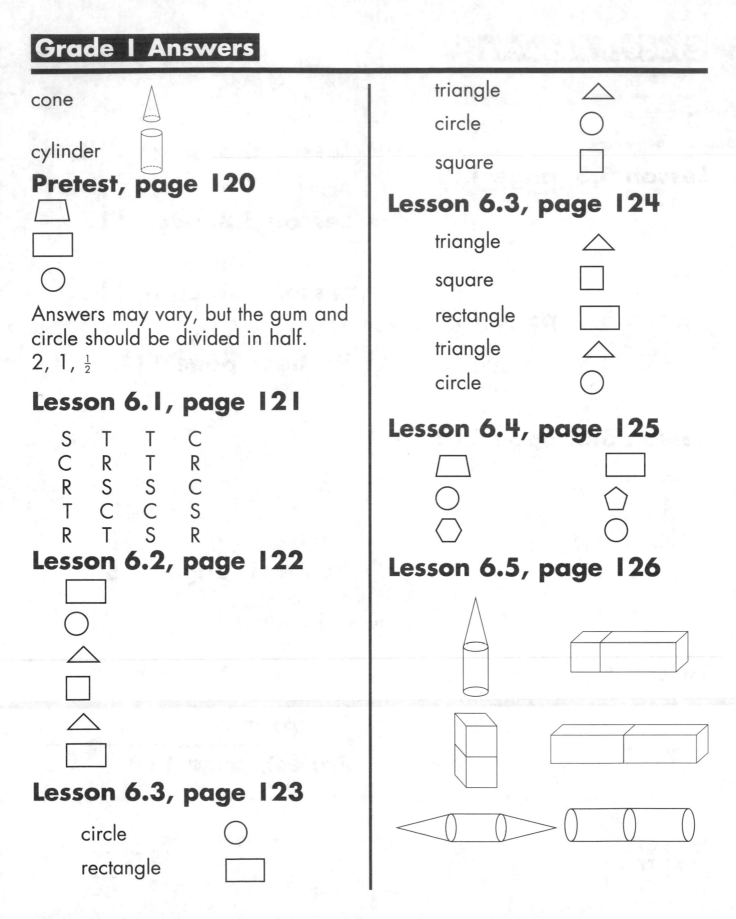

cylinder

Pretest, page 120

Answers may vary, but the gum and circle should be divided in half.
2, 1, $\frac{1}{2}$

Lesson 6.1, page 121

S	T	T	C
C	R	T	C
R	S	T	R
T	C	S	C
R	T	S	R

Lesson 6.2, page 122

Lesson 6.3, page 123

circle

rectangle

triangle

circle

square

Lesson 6.3, page 124

triangle

square

rectangle

triangle

circle

Lesson 6.4, page 125

Lesson 6.5, page 126

Grade 1 Answers

Lesson 6.6, page 127

Answers will vary but the apple and soap should be divided in half. Answers will vary but the rug and orange should be divided in thirds. Answers will vary but the pancake and coloring page should be divided in fourths.

Lesson 6.7, page 128

4, 1, $\frac{1}{4}$; 2, 1, $\frac{1}{2}$
2, 1, $\frac{1}{2}$; 4, 1, $\frac{1}{4}$
One-half; One-fourth

Posttest, page 129

square   cylinder   circle

R T C S R T

rectangular prism

circle

cone

Posttest, page 130

Answers will vary, but the rug should be divided into fourths.

4, 1, $\frac{1}{4}$; 4, 1, $\frac{1}{4}$

Final Test

Page 131

8	12	11	10	8	5
15	17	5	9	16	3
20	14	12	6	4	9
1	18	14	13	2	7
10	7	19	17	15	0
9	4	10	16	8	19
12	13	6	5	7	8

Page 132

9	8	9	6	1	3
7	8	2	15	8	2
4	6	7	3	1	9
0	9	7	6	1	2
6	7	13	9	0	3
3	2	8	4	4	0
6	8	1	17	6	0

Page 133

20; 11; 10; 16¢; 8; 12

Page 134

2¢; 8; 9; 18; 4; 9

Page 135

1	2	3	4	5	6	7	8	9	10
11	12	13	14	15	16	17	18	19	20
21	22	23	24	25	26	27	28	29	30
31	32	33	34	35	36	37	38	39	40
41	42	43	44	45	46	47	48	49	50
51	52	53	54	55	56	57	58	59	60
61	62	63	64	65	66	67	68	69	70
71	72	73	74	75	76	77	78	79	80
81	82	83	84	85	86	87	88	89	90
91	92	93	94	95	96	97	98	99	100
101	102	103	104	105	106	107	108	109	110
111	112	113	114	115	116	117	118	119	120

Grade 1 Answers

Page 136

35 < 36	64 > 44	13 < 23
73 > 37	98 > 89	41 > 14

2, 7, 27
4, 3, 43
3, 2, 32
1, 3, 13
87; 89
75; 39
54; 7
48; 25
31; 72

Page 137

5; 6; 9; 5

4:00	10:30
4 o'clock	10 thirty
8:00	9:30
8 o'clock	9 thirty

Page 138

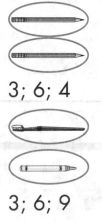

3; 6; 4

3; 6; 9

Page 139

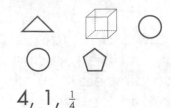

4, 1, $\frac{1}{4}$

Answers will vary, but the pancake should be divided into fourths.

Notes

Notes